Fly Fishing
New Jersey
Trout Streams

By
Matthew Grobert

Fly Fishing
New Jersey
Trout Streams

Matthew Grobert

Frank Amato
PORTLAND

Seek to understand – let passion be your guide.

For my children –
Megan, Matthew and Leigh
And
Debbie Foster

Acknowledgments

Much of what I have written here is the result of years of fly-fishing with a few very dedicated anglers who share my passion for our sport. Special thanks to my "Italian brother" Vincent Caffarra, whose modesty belies a great understanding of trout, insects, and angling. To Donald "Sam" Murnane, a great fishing companion and who in seeing this book is probably thinking "it's about damn time." And to Paul Santoriello, whose unending enthusiasm, energy, and not so subtle pushes kept me thinking about how to get here from there. And to Mark Newhouse, who gave me support and the opportunity to discover how I could combine my love of fly-fishing and writing to better educate not only myself, but many others in what for us may be the best use of our precious time on this earth. And lastly to my grandfather Harry J. Featherline, who never picked up a fly-rod yet taught me that no matter what life throws at you, one must persevere.

I also want to thank Kathy Hiserodt for her constant encouragement and patience. She read the first "rough" draft of each section and still managed to keep me on track with sound advice and thoughtful editing. If she ever decides to pick up a fly-rod, the trout better look out.

Once on the stream, I can only focus on the fish and the fishing, and so my thanks go to the angler/photographers who so generously contributed photographs so this book would be complete.

Also my thanks go to the many other anglers and friends who generously shared their methods, stories, theories, fly patterns, failures and successes.

Finally, a special thank you to my editor at Frank Amato Publications – Kim Koch – great job!

Published in 2007 by
Frank Amato Publications, Inc.
PO Box 82112 Portland, Oregon 97282 ◆ (503) 653-8108 www.amatobooks.com

All photos are the property of Matthew Grobert, unless otherwise noted.
Book Design by Lannie Alejandro Appel
Cover Photo by Mark Sagan ◆ Title Page Illustration by Michael Lipkin
Title Page Photograph by Jessica Lettich

Softbound: ISBN-13: 978-1-57188-417-6   Softbound UPC: 0-81127-00251-1
Printed in Hong Kong
1 3 5 7 9 10 8 6 4 2

contents

Sussex County wild-trout stream.

Sometimes I find it hard to believe that I have been trout fishing in New Jersey for 35 years. But I have been, and early on there was a period where I fished once or twice a week throughout the year. During the peak of the mayfly hatches—May and June—I would be out three or four times a week. I would leave work and go straight to the stream and fish until dark without stopping for dinner. I have to tell you that even now that I have slowed my pace the fishing has continually been good, and sometimes great, and there is always an opportunity to learn and grow both from a fishing standpoint and in a spiritual way. Fishing and appreciating nature has a way of balancing out the rest of my life.

I can remember the first trout I caught on a fly like it was yesterday, although I was 14 or 15 years old at the time. It was during a warm, humid evening in late May on the upper Passaic River in Millington. The river here is about twenty to twenty-five feet wide and was full of stocked trout and panfish. I learned early on that wading here was more of a hassle than a help, so I was fishing from shore. Most of the river bank is lined with trees and shrubs so you had to find an opening in the brush to make a proper back cast. Where there was no room for that, you used a sort of modified roll cast/flip cast to get your fly out to where the trout were holding.

The first hour or so I fished with a little ball of Velveeta cheese compressed around a size-twelve wet-fly hook and a small split-shot, six inches or so above on the leader. Yes, I was a cheese-baiter. I make no apologies for this as at the time fishing for me was all about catching fish and cheese was a magnet to stocked trout. Fortunately for me and the trout, after this evening on the water that all changed.

This was the standard operating procedure for me at that time. I would fish the cheese using my fly-rod and catch several trout before going to flies. That way I assured myself that there were trout in the river to be caught once I tied on a fly. It gave me the confidence necessary to switch to flies, being as green as I was to fly-fishing for trout. I really had no mentor, just friends that also liked to fish, but even they did not tie flies or fish with them. It was more of a fascination for them than something they really wanted to dive into. I also read everything I could get my hands on that had anything to do with fly-fishing.

So here I was standing on the bank of the Passaic River, fly-rod in hand peering into my box of freshly tied flies. I remember looking out over the river and seeing some caddis and a few small yellow mayflies in the air. On the water were more of the little yellow bugs. I concentrated on one that was floating across the way a foot or so off the bank. When it kicked into a ripple near a rock, BLIP! It was gone. A trout rose and took it like candy. I saw my first trout rise to a mayfly. My heart jumped and my mind went into overdrive.

Which fly should I tie on? A Black Gnat? A ratty looking Quill Gordon? I did not have any little yellow flies, or Sulphurs as we call them today. Which fly do I use? I looked and saw my favorite looking fly, a peacock-herl-bodied fly I had tied. I don't know if it had a name, but it was very cool looking; it had a red duck-quill tail, peacock herl body and furnace hackle and no wing. I grabbed it and tied it on my leader, a level leader of six-pound-test line about six feet long. The fish rose again and my adrenaline sped up.

Once I had the fly on I suddenly became focused and intent on doing what I needed to do to get my fly over that fish across the way. I remember looking back over my shoulder to make sure I could back cast just the way I did in my back yard. I whipped out some line and made a few false casts before dropping the rod tip and letting the line fall-out on the water in front of me. The fly landed about four feet short of my target, but I did get the feel of how the line would land and how I would have to keep it slightly upstream of my target to avoid drag.

I picked up the line and started the process all over again. Once I thought I had the right amount of line and leader extending out from the rod tip, I concentrated on a spot maybe eighteen inches above where the fish was rising. One last back cast and then a crisp, compact forward cast, my eyes on that spot the whole time. I dropped the rod tip, my line eased out and then dropped lightly on the water. My fly landed right where my gaze was focused. I could feel it, everything went as I envisioned it in my mind's eye.

The fly landed on its side and as if it were in slow motion, it drifted gently for a second or two and then it disappeared in a loud SIP! The trout took my fly! Somehow I stayed focused and tightened the line while lifting my rod tip and I had it hooked. It jumped once right after I set the hook, and then it dogged in the midstream current as I tried to gain line on it. In a few minutes I had my line/leader connection in the rod tip and I netted the fish in front of me. It was an eleven-inch-long, pink-striped, black-speckled rainbow trout, the fly firmly in the corner of its jaw. I was hooked and the cheese was history.

This book contains the lessons learned over my thirty-something years of experience since that day of fly-fishing in New Jersey's rivers and streams. The first thing I would like to point out is that this is not the complicated sport some make it out to be. It is really quite simple if you allow it to be. Of course, there are some anglers that can't help but go overboard and more power to them if they are having fun. It is all about understanding the fish, the rivers, and the many creatures within them that the trout feed on. Yes, it's a lot of information, but it will come to you as you fish and experience the varied conditions and moods of the wonderful rivers winding their way through New Jersey.

Prequest River

New Jersey Trout Streams

Whether it is a small, crystal-clear wild-trout stream winding its way through a mixed grove of hardwood trees, hemlocks and boulders, or a medium sized river meandering through a valley surrounded by cornfields and cows, it can be found in New Jersey. In fact, New Jersey is full of freestone trout streams of varying sizes throughout the northern half of the state just waiting for an angler to cast his fly. Over 500 miles of these trout streams have water quality that supports year-round trout survival; many of these streams boast natural trout reproduction—wild trout. In addition, the New Jersey State Division of Fish and Wildlife utilizes the Pequest Trout Hatchery to stock over 350 miles of trout streams in the spring and fall months with brook, brown, and rainbow trout.

Although most of these trout streams are found in the less populated areas of northern and western New Jersey, many can be found within 25 miles of New York City, including several wild-trout streams. Just about every river and stream in New Jersey is a freestone river.

A freestone river has a bed primarily made up of gravel, stones, and boulders, which when floods and high water occur move, forming the pools and changing runs that are necessary for good trout habitat. The pools can be quite deep and well

defined, while runs are wide with low banks in most cases. Freestone rivers are fed by rainfall, snowmelt, and mountain springs. I should also tell you that freestone rivers generally have high temperature fluctuations throughout the year, which can affect their ability to hold trout all year round, particularly in hot summers. These waters range in size from narrow, swift, tumbling mountain streams to larger rivers that average 30 feet wide—some wider in their lower reaches.

In all, there are 35 designated wild-trout streams in the state that receive no trout stocking. Most of these gems are quite small, averaging perhaps 6-8 feet across. Some can be found in urban locales while others will be found in the rocky, forested mountains of the northwestern part of the state. These stream hold some of the most beautiful, stream-bred fish you have ever seen. Most of these trout average only 6 inches in length, but they more than make up for it with their vibrant colors, delicate speckles, and perfectly formed fins.

New Jersey also has less than a half dozen streams that have limestone, or spring creek characteristics. A spring creek is primarily fed by springs that well up from deep in limestone beds. Very little of their water comes from rainfall which make them less prone to flooding. Because their water comes from deep in the earth, its temperature is fairly consistent throughout the year and because the rock through which it flows purifies it, it is quite clear. Spring creeks also tend to be overgrown with willows and other vegetation that stabilizes the banks, but can wreak havoc on the fly-fisherman by making stalking, casting, and fighting fish a challenge. Most will also contain large mats of watercress or other water vegetation throughout their length that are divided by the narrow bands of clear water where the current is strongest. Talk about a challenging environment to fish in!

While the state must rely on stocking to maintain the trout populations in most New Jersey rivers and streams, you might be surprised at how many of these stocked streams also have naturally reproducing trout in them. A 2004 study showed that there are about 123 streams that have naturally reproducing brook trout, 79 streams with naturally reproducing brown trout, and about 18 streams in the state with naturally reproducing rainbow trout. The brook trout is native to New Jersey and has been designated the state fish.

Like most states in the mid-Atlantic region, New Jersey's trout fishing season gets under way in April. Opening day is usually the second Saturday of April after which the state operates a weekly in-season trout-stocking program through the end of May, as this is the height of trout fishing activity. But because New Jersey has a relatively mild climate most of the year, the dedicated fly-fisher can fish for trout just about year round. In the summertime, trout fishing activity does slow as high air temperatures during the day can make the fish and angler alike quite sluggish.

In the fall when things begin to cool down, trout fishing activity increases. Many anglers think this is the best time of the year to fish because the trout are active and there are fewer fishermen than in the spring. And thankfully, the state also has a fall stocking schedule to accommodate those hardy anglers that don't let the cold keep them inside. Winter trout stream fishing usually occurs into December and stops for most in January and February, but depending on the weather in some years you can fish right through the season as little ice forms streamside.

That should give you a general idea of what trout fishing in New Jersey is all about. In the next chapter is some background on some of the more popular rivers and streams in the state. I should note that even though these are the more popular streams in the state, solitude can be found with a little exploration and legwork. And if that does not do it for you, there are always the smaller less popular waters and wild-trout streams.

What follows each description of the river is a hatch chart showing only the insects that hatch consistently from year to year on that particular river. It should be noted that most, if not all of these streams, have hatches of other less common mayflies, caddisflies, and other aquatic insects that come off them during the year. In particular, you will find that on most evenings during the warmer months of the year there will be some kind of caddis in the air and/or on the water. These hatches do bring up trout to feed on the surface, but in a much less predictable manner. Also, some sections of these rivers will have good hatches of a certain bug while other sections none. This can depend on a variety of factors from water quality, water type (i.e. some mayfly nymphs don't like fast water), and water temperature. The more you fish a particular stream, the more you will learn its secrets, and that's what fly-fishing is all about.

The last thing I want to do before we move on is get on my soapbox and remind you that the rivers and streams belong to all of us. When you encounter others on the stream be courteous and give them elbow room. Do not try to fish the same water someone else is, even if they are catching fish and you are not. If you see an angler working his way upstream of downstream, do not hop in the water just ahead of him. Move up or down stream a pool or two. The bottom line here is the good old golden rule—think about how you expect another angler to respect your space on the stream and do the same for them. And not everyone is a talker, so if you think you may be bothering someone by talking to them while they are fishing, you probably are. They aren't angry, they just want solitude. Do not take it personally.

The same rule applies to private property, the environment and anything else that is not yours. Bring out what you bring in whether its trash, used tippet or an old leader you removed from your rig. Respect private property and make sure you park your vehicle in a legal place that does not block someone in or damage landscaping.

Okay, I'm done preaching. Go forth and have fun and be careful, and don't forget to catch some fish and leave some for another day. As Lee Wulff once said, "The fish you release may be a gift to another fisherman as it may have been a gift to you." There's nothing wrong with keeping a couple if you are going to eat them, but once you catch and keep your fill, practice catch and release.

Photo by Ralph Ford

Wild-trout stream in winter.

Wild New Jersey brook trout.

Photo by Mark Sagan

New Jersey Trout

Brook Trout

The brook trout, the state fish of New Jersey, is the only trout that is native to the state. In select streams it continues to thrive naturally although these fish tend to be on the smaller side, averaging six inches in length. There are about 123 streams that have naturally reproducing brook trout populations. The NJ Division of Fish and Wildlife also stocks well over 200,000 brook trout in rivers, streams, and lakes throughout the state that average over ten inches in length. There are a number of rivers that are stocked with brook trout that also sustain a healthy natural population as well.

The brook trout is one of the most beautiful fish found in North America. Its back is dark olive green with lighter worm-like markings. Its sides lighten to a bluish green speckled by tan markings and small red dots that are surrounded by pale blue halos, and the belly is white. The lower fins have a bright white front edge which is separated from the reddish orange fin by a black line. The tail is not forked and rather square. During breeding season the males turn a bright orange on their lower sides and belly.

Brook trout require cool, clean water to survive and therefore they are an indicator of good water quality. They are voracious feeders that will eat everything from worms and nymphs to small fish, crayfish, and any terrestrial insects unlucky enough to land on the water near one.

Brook trout are considered to be the least wary of the trout and therefore the easiest to catch. When hooked they tend to dig towards the bottom and muscle their way into deadfalls or under rocks and overhanging banks, and they rarely leap from the water.

Rainbow Trout

The rainbow trout is native only to the North American west coast watersheds from northern Mexico to Alaska. However, it has been stocked throughout the country for over a century and continues to be one of the most sought after freshwater game fish. In New Jersey, some of these trout have managed to breed naturally and now there are about 18 streams that have self-sustaining populations of rainbow trout. These wild fish tend to be on the smaller size, and like the brook trout only average about 6-7 inches in

length at maturity. The NJ Division of Fish and Game manages to stock over 200,000 rainbow trout every year throughout the state giving the angler plenty of opportunities to pursue for this wonderful game fish.

The coloration of the rainbow trout varies greatly depending on the strain and/or the hatchery it came from. Their back will range in color from a silvery gray to a dark grayish olive that lightens as it goes down the sides of the fish and is covered with small black spots. The lateral line from just behind the gills to the tail may be a dull pink or a bright reddish pink, or any color in between; this is where it gets its name. Wild rainbow trout tend to be much more consistent in coloration with a gray olive back that lightens to an almost amber olive, and a soft pink lateral line with light indigo vertical parr markings. The belly of wild fish is usually white.

Rainbow trout prefer cold, flowing water with stone and boulder covered bottoms with deep pools and lots of overhead cover for shade and protection. They will also be found in very fast pocket water behind rocks and ledges. They are known for their hard-fighting agility and tendency to leap from the water when hooked. Rainbow trout also possess what is referred to as

A typical New Jersey wild rainbow trout.

Wild brown trout.

"Distant Touch" sense. This is the ability to feel distant vibrations through its lateral line 800 times that of man. What this means for the angler is that a stealthy approach is paramount when wading a river; lift and move your feet carefully so as not to kick or grind the rocks and gravel on the stream bottom.

Brown Trout

The brown trout is a native of Europe and western Asia that was successfully transplanted in North America around 1883. It is a well-known fact that this is by far the most difficult of the trout to catch—they are extremely wary—and therefore are an ideal quarry for the fly-fisherman. Brown trout are very hardy and able to adapt well to habitat degradation and changes in their environment, making them the ideal trout to stock late in the season. The NJ Division of Fish and Wildlife stocks about 150,000 brown trout every year that average about eleven inches in length. The brown trout naturally reproduces in about 79 New Jersey streams.

Brown trout coloration ranges from a dark golden brown to light bronze on its back that lightens as you move down its flanks to the belly. It will have anywhere from a few to many large black spots and a few bright red ones scattered about. The fins are amber and the belly is usually a pale yellow to white. As the fish grows in size its coloration lightens and the black spots dominate its sides and take on a cross-like shape while the red spots tend to disappear altogether.

While the rainbow trout has "Distant Touch" sense, the brown trout has a specialized retina that allows it to see very well in low light conditions. For this reason browns will tend to hang out beneath undercut banks, deadfalls, and vegetation during the day to shield its eyes from the bright sun. This explains why many of the anglers that fish for large browns at night are so successful. Brown trout have a tendency to dominate their environment and will be found in the prime lies of a particular pool or run. And because brown trout can tolerate warmer water and are more aggressive than our native brook trout, they will out-compete the native fish whenever their habitat is disrupted. They feed on invertebrates and airborne insects and as they grow in size they will eat crayfish, minnows, and even small trout.

Tackle for New Jersey Trout Streams

The subject of what tackle to use for a given situation is one that has long been debated among serious fly-fisherman. Still, it is not rocket science by any stretch of the imagination. While I would never try to tell you what the perfect outfit is, I will try to keep this simple and tell you what I would recommend for the average angler fly-fishing the rivers and streams of New Jersey. In the end, it is you that has to be most comfortable with the equipment you are using, and therefore, use the following only as an accurate guideline.

We will start with the rod, reel, and line and go from there. The rod should be 8 to 8 1/2 feet in length for a 5-weight floating line. How many pieces it is, is up to the individual angler and whether they plan on traveling to distant rivers with it. This will permit you to throw good sized streamers and weighted nymphs, while also being light enough to be comfortable while fishing even the tiniest dry flies. The line is also heavy enough to handle light to moderate winds without too much difficulty. For the reel, you could spend $35, or you could spend $300, that's

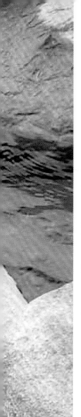

up to you and your budget. The bottom line is that it should hold the 5-weight line and 75 to 100 yards of 20-pound backing without the line binding when it is completely wound on the spool.

You will also need a pair of waders, or at least hip boots, for wading when the weather and water are too cold to wet wade. I have done just fine over the last 10 years or so with waist-high stocking-foot waders. For warmth there is neoprene, and if you want to go light I would recommend breathable waders. Keep in mind with breathable waders you just need to add layers underneath—polypropylene or fleece—and they work well even in the cold. Like rods and reels you can spend around a hundred dollars on them, or hundreds of dollars. The boots you wear will be as important as staying dry as they must be sturdy and at least have felt or some type of non-slip surface to provide traction on underwater rocks and stones. For added traction you may want studded felt soles for another layer of protection in fast or heavy water. I have been using felt soles for years in New Jersey and I've never had a problem, but that may change as I grow long in the tooth and become less agile.

For your tackle—fly boxes, leader material, tools and other necessities depending on your love of gadgets and such—you have a wide variety of choices. There are all kinds of vests made for these things, some light-weight and others that have enough pockets and zippers to stock a fly shop in. You can also get these neat tackle packs and hip packs for your tackle. This is what I use. I just sling it over my shoulder and keep the pack itself on my back except when I need something in it. It's out of the way and there's nothing in front of me when I am fishing that might catch my line at a critical moment. Bottom line here, the choice is yours; fly-fishing is a very democratic sport indeed.

What else is there? I would recommend the following should be part of your tackle; whether it be in a vest or tackle pack, you will need these things: forceps, nippers, spare leaders, tippet material, split-shot (non-lead), dry-fly floatant, and a hook sharpener. This last item is probably the single most overlooked item. I don't know if it's because anglers do not realize how important it is, or if they just think their hooks stay sharp no matter what. What I can tell you is that I sharpen the hook on the fly I am using every 4-6 casts if it's a nymph, wet, or streamer; and I check my dry-fly hook every so often as well because you never know and you do not want to miss a hook-up with the trout of a lifetime because you couldn't be bothered to sharpen your hook. You would be amazed at how quickly a trout and can suck in and spit out your fly, particularly a nymph, without the angler even feeling it. When hook is razor sharp all it has to do is touch an area of the mouth or jaw when this happens and it will stick, when it's dull, it will just touch and keep going. Think about it, your nymph is bouncing along a stream bottom covered with stones and rocks and every one of them that the point of the hook hits can dull it. Use a hook sharpener and I guarantee you will hook more fish.

The leaders and tippet material you will want to carry are important. There will be times when you will need to replace the entire leader. And the tippet is for lengthening the leader when it gets cut back from changing flies, and for when a particular situation calls for a lighter or heavier tippet. I would recommend the following for spare leaders: 7 1/2-foot 4X and 5X, 9-foot 4X, 5X and 6X, and 12-foot 5X, 6X and maybe 7X if you fish tiny flies in clear water. The tippet material you carry should be on spools and you want to have 3X down to 7X; you will probably use the 4X and 5X the most.

The style and type of fly boxes you use is completely up to you. There are dozens of sizes, styles, and types. I use ripple foam boxes for my nymphs and streamers, and compartment boxes for my dries, this keeps them from getting crushed. Find what you like and go for it.

As for the flies you should have, read on, have fun, and good luck.

*Trout Conservation Area of the South Branch of the Raritan River,
better known as the Claremont Stretch.*

New Jersey Trout Fishing Regulations

The following is a basic summary of the New Jersey trout fishing regulations in effect at the time of this writing. While many of these regulations have been in effect for many years, they are subject to change. For up-to-date information and additional regulations, consult the New Jersey Division of Fish and Wildlife Website www.njfishandwildlife.com

Opening day for trout is usually the second Saturday in April and the season runs until the following year Sunday that is three weeks before the next opening day. The season is closed on all trout-stocked waters during this three-week period with the exception of some of the special regulation waters. Anyone between the ages of 16 and 69 must have a New Jersey fishing license and trout stamp to fish for trout. The State of New Jersey stocks approximately 350 miles of rivers and streams with trout in the spring—April and May. The state also has a fall stocking program that includes the major trout streams and other popular waters that usually takes place in October as long as water levels permit.

The size limit throughout the year on streams where general regulations apply is 7 inches. Between January 1 and the Sunday 3 weeks before

opening day the daily creel limit is 4 trout. From the second Saturday in April until May 31, the daily creel limit is 6 trout. From June 1 to December 31 the daily creel limit is reduced to 4 trout. Waters with in-season stocking closures are closed to fishing from 5:00 a.m. until 5:00 p.m. on the days listed for stocking by the Division of Fish and Wildlife. As of this writing there are 16 rivers and streams that have in-season stocking closure days. Consult the Division's Summary of Freshwater Fishing Regulations or Website for further information and dates.

There also dozens of other rivers and streams that are stocked with trout that do not have in-season stocking dates. They are listed by County in the Division's Summary of Freshwater Fishing Regulations and on their Website.

Special Regulation Trout Areas

Year-Round Trout Conservation Areas: These river sections have a minimum size limit of 15 inches, and daily creel limit of 1 trout. During the three-week pre-season stocking period in the spring these waters are catch & release only.

Only artificial lures may be used; no live or preserved bait or any natural or synthetic substance that contains a bait scent may be used.

At the time of this writing the following four rivers have sections with this designation: **East Branch Paulinskill River, South Branch of the Raritan River** (2 separate sections), and **Toms River**.

Seasonal Trout Conservation Areas: These river sections have the same regulations as those above except during the first six weeks of the trout fishing season—beginning the second Saturday in April at 8:00 a.m. During this six-week period there are no gear restrictions on these waters and the minimum size limit is 7 inches, and the daily creel limit is 6 trout. On in-season stocking dates, fishing is not permitted on the Pequest and Musconetcong rivers until 5:00 p.m.

At the time of this writing the following rivers have sections with this designation: **Pequannock River**, **Pequest River**, and **Musconetcong River**.

Fly-Fishing Areas: These river sections are restricted to the use of artificial flies only. No lures or bait are permitted. Spinning reels or other angling whereby a fly is cast directly from the reel is prohibited. During the three-week pre-season stocking period, fishing is not permitted. The minimum size limit is 7 inches, and the daily creel limit during the first 6 weeks of the season is 6 trout; at all other times the daily creel limit is 4 trout.

At the time of this writing the following rivers have sections with this designation: **Big Flat Brook River**, and the **Blewett Tract** – a 0.5 mile section of the **Big Flat Brook River** - During the first 8 days of the season – from opening day until the following Monday at 5 a.m. – gear restrictions do not apply on the Blewett Tract.

The Division of Fish and Wildlife publishes a complete list of all New Jersey waters that are stocked with trout along with all applicable statutes, codes and regulations. There are actually two lists; one that lists the rivers that have closed stocking dates and the dates they are closed, and the other that lists the rivers that have no closed stocking dates – this list shows how many times the river is stocked during the stocking season.

A) Big Flatbrook
B) Paulinskill River
C) Pequest River
D) Musconetcong River
E) South Branch of Raritan River
F) Black River/Lamington River
G) North Branch of Raritan River
H) Passaic River
I) Rockaway River
J) Pequannock River
K) Ramapo River
L) Toms River

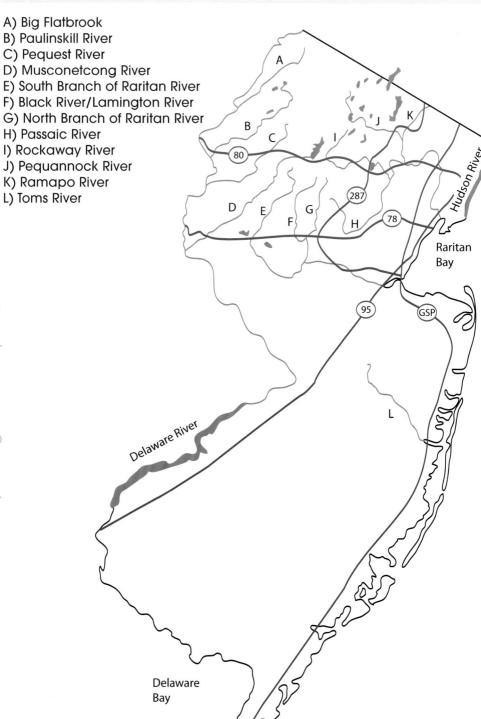

Fly Fishing New Jersey Trout Streams

An angler works the Big Flatbrook River on an autumn afternoon.

Photo by Greg Sabol

New Jersey Rivers

Big Flatbrook

(See river map on page 74)

In the northwestern part of New Jersey there flows one of the best and most scenic freestone trout streams in the state. It tumbles and flows for 15 miles through thick forest in some sections, and farmland long since left to fallow in others. Its water is clear and clean, giving the angler a good view of the bottom and the fish a good view of the angler if he is not careful. It is characterized by many different water types throughout its length – riffles and runs in one section, pocket water in another, gravel bottom runs, and deep pools laden with silted floors.

The Big Flatbrook is very angler friendly, having more public access than any other trout stream in the state. Additionally, it seems that every run, pocket and pool holds a trout or two, and sometimes many more as it flows southward to the Delaware River. Because it flows primarily through State Forest land and Wildlife Management Areas, the land surrounding the river is unfettered by homes or other signs of civilization. Although the Flatbrook is stocked by the state, it does support a good population of stream-bred trout.

19

The upper part of the Big Flatbrook, above Route 206, is a relatively small mountain stream with mostly pocket water and riffles. The few pools in this section are on the small side as the river averages 15-20 feet across. The river is surrounded and shaded by thick forest immediately above Route 206 that help keep it cool, even in the heat of summer. These same trees also force the angler to be creative when casting, as there is little room for a back cast. Even here though there are some stretches that flow lazily through open fields. Fortunately though this is the coolest part of New Jersey—the highlands—so when the daytime temperatures do get high, things cool off a lot and quickly late in the day for a good 12 hours even in the summer months.

The section of the Big Flatbrook from the Route 206 Bridge downstream to the Mountain Road Bridge has been designated as a Fly Fishing Only stretch. Think four miles of beautiful water with nice pools, pocket water and long riffles that harbor plenty of trout and the insects they feed on. Within this stretch, the Little Flatbrook enters the Big Flatbrook and the river changes character as it gains in volume from the added water. The river widens and the pools are bigger and deeper, as are the riffles and pocket water, which increases the available holding water for trout. If you look at the river on Google Earth, you will see that the river widens significantly here. This allows the fish to survive and hold-over even in very hot summers and cold winters. For the fly-fisherman, this is New Jersey's nirvana. Also within this stretch, there is a clearly marked, half-mile section called the Blewett Tract that has some added regulations that apply to it. Be sure you check the regulations that are posted along this stretch to be sure you are fishing legally.

The lower section of the river is fairly large, averaging 50 feet across, with big, deep pools and nice runs ideal for the fly-fisherman. Sussex County Route 615 parallels the river here giving the angler plenty of areas to park and then wade up or downstream. The hatches here are as good as they get and the pools hold some good-sized trout. That doesn't mean you won't have to work for your fish most days because most of them are browns that demand your fly acts like the naturals it feeds on. And if you want really big fish, drag a streamer, Woolly Bugger, or crayfish imitation through the deeper holes early or late in the day and you might just find out how big some of the trout get in this river.

The Big Flatbrook is classic trout water much like its bigger cousins a short way north in the Catskill Mountains. You can truly get lost in the moment here as you are surrounded by cool, clear

Big Flatbrook Primary Hatches

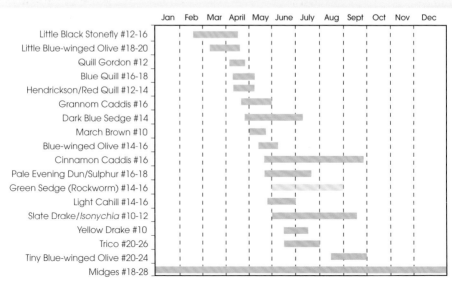

water bordered by hardwood trees, hemlocks and shrubs left to grow naturally after their caretaker farmers abandoned their plows. When the fishing is slow here I find myself picking out the sounds of songbirds attracted to the river's edge, perhaps for the same reasons I am there. Do they admire the little speckled wild trout along with the angler just before he releases it back into the river?

Hatches on the Flatbrook are varied and consistent with both mayfly and caddis hatches occurring throughout the spring to fall season. The mayfly hatches are very good with the Hendrickson, Sulphur, Light Cahill, Trico and *Isonychia* hatches being the most prolific. Caddis hatches can be quite heavy as well at times with the various species of the cinnamon caddis hatching to some degree from spring to September. The Grannom caddis hatches in good numbers in the early season starting with the darker species and ending with the lighter, green-bodied variety so well matched by a #16 Henryville Caddis dry.

The Trico hatch on the Big Flatbrook is as good as it is anywhere in the East, occurring from the middle of June through July. The hatch/spinner falls may start as early as sun up in the hotter periods, but in June or during cooler periods you can have good Trico fishing from sunrise until 9 a.m. Both the wild trout and the now river-wizened stocked fish will feed on them with abandon in the first few weeks of the hatch. As the days grow warmer and the trout see every conceivable Trico imitation and presentation, they get fussy and nothing but the best cast/presentation and lightest leaders (7X or 8X) will take fish.

Access to the Big Flatbrook is good all along its length. County Roads 615 and 640 run track the river in the lower half, and the upper half can be hiked up into from the Route 206 Bridge parking area.

Paulinskill River

(See river map on page 75)

The Paulinskill River starts out as two small streams, the East and West branches, that come together in Warbasse Junction just south of the town of Lafayette in Northern Sussex County. The West Branch of the Paulinskill is a relatively short stream that starts as the outlet of a small lake just north of Newton. In contrast the East Branch starts in the hills a ways

Photo by Jerry VanNest

The Paulinskill in early summer.

north and easy of Newton as a mountain stream. The east branch is fed by springs along its way that squeeze their way up through limestone, which nourishes it and helps create ideal trout habitat. Once the two branches do meet, the Paulinskill is a small crystal-clear creek winding its way through the rolling hills and old farmland typical of this part of New Jersey on its way south and west to the Delaware River.

Before I move on with the main Paulinskill River, I should mention that a section of the East Branch is a Year Round Trout Conservation Area. This section begins at the Limecrest railroad spur bridge and goes downstream a distance of about 2.25 miles to its junction with the West Branch of the Paulinskill. The 2.25 miles is a figure the Division's Trout Fishing Regulations give and I believe are as the crow flies, the actual river length is considerably more as it twists back and forth like a dark, watery serpent throughout most of the Conservation Area. You will find a mix of stream-bred brown and brook trout here, some whose vibrant colors will stay with the angler long after they release them back into the clear waters from whence they came.

The upper main Paulinskill has limited access as much of this water is posted and off limits to the public until you get near the hamlet of Marksboro. The water that is open to fishing in this upper section offers some fine small-stream fly-fishing opportunities for both stocked and stream-bred trout. A short, light-line fly rod and a handful of terrestrial patterns on a summer evening on the river here will quickly wipe away your cares and bring you back to earth.

Once you get below Marksboro, more of the river becomes accessible, and as you approach the

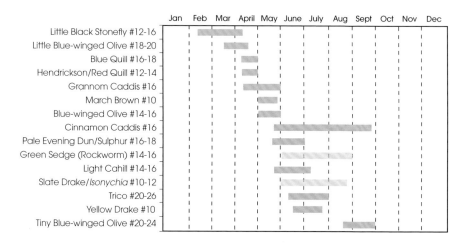

	Jan	Feb	Mar	April	May	June	July	Aug	Sept	Oct	Nov	Dec
Little Black Stonefly #12-16		▨										
Little Blue-winged Olive #18-20			▨									
Blue Quill #16-18				▨								
Hendrickson/Red Quill #12-14				▨								
Grannom Caddis #16				▨								
March Brown #10					▨							
Blue-winged Olive #14-16					▨							
Cinnamon Caddis #16						▨▨▨						
Pale Evening Dun/Sulphur #16-18						▨						
Green Sedge (Rockworm) #14-16						▨▨▨						
Light Cahill #14-16						▨						
Slate Drake/*Isonychia* #10-12						▨▨▨						
Trico #20-26							▨▨					
Yellow Drake #10							▨					
Tiny Blue-winged Olive #20-24								▨				

Blairstown region fewer and fewer stretches are posted. The river here is characterized by long, slow pools separated by pocket water and fast runs. The width of the river varies greatly here depending on the terrain from 30 feet up to as much as about 60 feet. The hatches here are good and the state stocks the river with plenty of trout. The trout hold-over well here and good trout fishing can be had throughout the year in this section of the river. There is also a respectable population of wild trout here, some of which grow to good sizes.

Near Blairstown and downstream, access is as easy as parking and fishing in many places. In the town itself where the river bisects a park, the water can be crowded, especially during the early spring season. There is plenty of water though and a short drive up or down river and/or some leg work will find you solitude. Here the Paulinskill has long pools separated by mild riffles and short runs, and a few sharp curves with deep undercut banks along the outside. Below the town, access can be gained by way of Sipley Road and Airport Road.

As you go down river from town on Route 94, the river widens and slows some, but the fishing remains good all the way to Columbia Lake, just a short distance from the Delaware River. Although Route 94 does not exactly parallel the river, it does follow along enough that most cross roads leading south traverse the river making for good access. And there is some nice water here with good hatches and pools and runs tailor-made for dry-fly fishing.

The Paulinskill has very good hatches of Hendricksons, Sulphurs and small late-season blue-winged olives, as well as other mayflies such as the Trico that hatch in numbers sufficient enough to produce good dry-fly fishing. If the mayflies do not cooperate, there are hatches of caddis almost every day from April to September. Most notably there is the early season Grannom, the various cinnamon caddis species that come off for several months, and many other lesser species that come off throughout the warmer months. Early season, or rather pre-season, can bring very good action when the little black stoneflies break out just as winter starts to lose its grip on the land.

Pequest River
(See river map on page 76)

The Pequest is one of those rivers it takes some time for the fly-fisherman to get to know. It doesn't give up its secrets in just one or two outings, and even after you do have some experience on it, it can drive you crazy some days. But it is well worth the time of getting to know it because it has good access, offers solitude, and it tends to have plenty of large fish. It also has some of the best hatches of any New Jersey trout stream.

The Pequest River is one that is very inviting to the angler. For starters, it has all kinds of holding water; fast riffles, pocket water, stone-filled runs, deep pools, and slow weedy sections that harbor tons of invertebrates for its trout to feed on. Unless

A lone angler nymphs the Pequest River.

you fish near the hatchery, you can find solitude in most sections just by taking a short hike up or down stream from your car. Access is not a problem at all as Route 46 runs alongside the river for much of its length.

I will break the river down into three sections to describe it—above the hatchery, the hatchery section, and below the hatchery—as that is how most anglers know it. The water above the hatchery, from Great Meadow downstream to the Conservation Area, has a lot of nice smooth runs that slow and deepen to pools, with pocket water in between the runs. Most of this water is well shaded by stands of trees that help keep it sheltered and cool. Above Great Meadows the river has little holding water for trout and it gets very shallow when rain is scarce.

The hatchery section is well marked and is easily accessed as the state has constructed a good-sized parking lot near to the river. The lot is off the same road that leads to the hatchery. Here the river

averages 20-30 feet across. It is designated a Seasonal Trout Conservation Area beginning at the Conrail bridge upstream of the hatchery and ending 1.6 miles downstream at the Route 625 bridge (Pequest Furnace Road). This section gets lots of pressure because it always has fish in it and many of them are large. It also has a good hold-over population of trout. These fish can be very fickle at times as they see every fly ever conceived by fly tiers. Don't expect to fish alone if you decide to hit this stretch when the weather is anything but nasty or very cold.

The water below the Hatchery/Conservation Area all the way to the Delaware River is as good as it is anywhere on the river. There are some wonderful pools that are tailor-made for the dry-fly fisherman with good hatches and plenty of trout. The river gets larger here, averaging about 40 feet across; some stretches are as wide as 50 feet across. This section also fishes well when water levels drop in the late spring and summer, although the water does get crystal clear making the trout especially wary.

The Pequest has some very good hatches throughout the main season – March through September – and excellent midge hatches all year. Like most of the other major New Jersey rivers it has reliable annual hatches of Hendrickson and Sulphur mayflies, a few significant caddis species, a couple of which hatch sporadically throughout the warmer months, and a very good early-season stonefly hatch.

New Jersey Rivers

Pequest River Primary Hatches

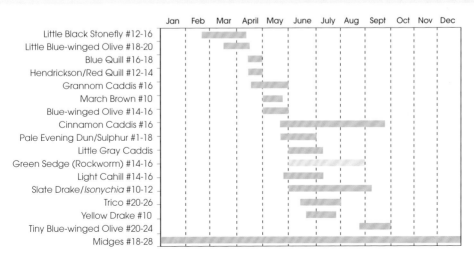

The Musconetcong River at Point Mountain.

Musconetcong River

(See river map on page 77)

The Musconetcong River, or "Musky" as anglers know it, is one of New Jersey's larger trout rivers, averaging 30-40 feet in width throughout most of its length. It is heavily stocked, yet in some sections naturally reproducing trout can be found, most of these are brook trout with an occasional wild brown trout being caught. Because of its size, the Musky has a good population of hold-over trout in many sections, especially those that run through less populated regions.

Quality trout fishing begins in the upper end of the Musky just below Saxton Falls. Here the river offers the angler wide pools, deep runs and riffles bordered by large trees. Already fairly wide with deep pools and runs, the river holds good numbers of both wild trout and stocked fish. This section flows down into Stephens State Park above the town of Hackettstown where access is excellent on both sides of the river. There are deep pools and nice pocket water throughout the park that hold trout year round. I have had some good days in late winter here when the sun was bright and the water clear, fishing little black stonefly imitations on top. Stoneflies are plentiful in the park water and the angler would be wise to carry some rather large stone nymphs in brown and/or black to ply the water when nothing is working on top. The trout are very accustomed to seeing these nymphs, some as large as 2 inches long.

As the Musky enters Hackettstown it slows somewhat and is characterized by long pools separated by riffles and pocket water. The river is quite wide as it meanders through the farmlands giving the angler plenty of room to stalk and cast to fish. This area also has abundant weed growth in some sections that support a wide variety of invertebrates while offering safe harbor for its trout.

Route 57 parallels the river from Hackettstown down river to Penwell offering plenty of access along the way. Here the Musky flows alternately through farmland and wooded areas and offers easy wading and lots of room for your back cast. Many of the pools are long and moderate in flow, making for some terrific dry-fly fishing when the trout are feeding on top. The section of the river that winds through Beattystown area, which is about halfway between Hackettstown and Penwell, is especially angler-friendly water. It is heavily stocked in spring and fall and has a good population of hold-over fish. This water also has good hatches of Hendricksons, Sulphurs and Tricos, with fairly consistent hatches of blue-winged olives in spring and fall.

As you head south from Beattystown on Route 57, if you make a left onto Penwell Road and go a short ways you will come to the Penwell Bridge. From here downstream about one mile to the Point Mountain Bridge, the Musky is designated a Seasonal Trout Conservation Area.

The river tightens a bit through this stretch creating some nice pools and holding water that have good flows and healthy populations of both mayflies and caddis.

As you go downstream from the Point Mountain Bridge and conservation stretch there is some posted land but for the most part there is good access. There is open water in the towns of Hampton and Asbury and then as you go downstream there are a few private clubs. The water that is open in this section of the river has a good population of stream-bred trout—mostly brook trout—and a good number of the club-

Musconetcong River

stocked fish migrate into these waters. It is worthwhile to scout the open water down here as the hatches are good and in the warmer months you can enjoy some terrific late-day dry-fly fishing with caddis and mayfly spinners.

The lower section of the Musconetcong, from Route 78 Bloomsbury down to Riegelsville where it enters the Delaware River, is a fairly large river. There are many stretches of river here that have public access and the fishing is good although a little tougher because there is more water to read. On the plus side, fishing pressure is relatively light compared to the more popular areas up river. Some might think there are less fish here and that's why there are fewer anglers, but that is not the case. I believe it is more a matter of the bigger water being less inviting and seemingly more difficult. This area is best fished by breaking it down into a series of smaller streams and fishing each section as though that were the case. There are some big trout in this section.

Hatches? What doesn't hatch on the Musky? I've seen just about every common mayfly and caddisfly come off this river over the 30 years I have been fishing it. Some come off in very good numbers and others come off in dribs and drabs or only in certain sections. The reality is that this is the case on most of the major New Jersey rivers and streams, only I have noticed it more on the Musky because it's the river on which I

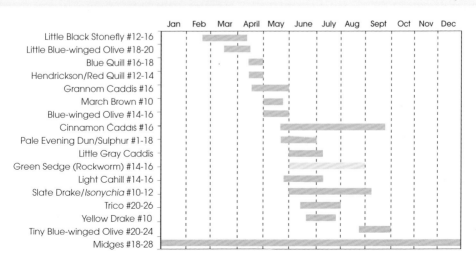

Musconetcong River Primary Hatches

	Jan	Feb	Mar	April	May	June	July	Aug	Sept	Oct	Nov	Dec
Little Black Stonefly #12-16		▨	▨									
Little Blue-winged Olive #18-20		▨	▨									
Blue Quill #16-18				▨								
Hendrickson/Red Quill #12-14				▨								
Grannom Caddis #16				▨	▨							
March Brown #10					▨							
Blue-winged Olive #14-16					▨							
Cinnamon Caddis #16					▨	▨	▨	▨	▨			
Pale Evening Dun/Sulphur #1-18					▨	▨	▨					
Little Gray Caddis						▨	▨					
Green Sedge (Rockworm) #14-16					▨	▨	▨	▨	▨			
Light Cahill #14-16					▨	▨	▨					
Slate Drake/*Isonychia* #10-12					▨	▨	▨	▨	▨			
Trico #20-26						▨	▨	▨				
Yellow Drake #10						▨	▨					
Tiny Blue-winged Olive #20-24								▨	▨			
Midges #18-28	▨	▨	▨	▨	▨	▨	▨	▨	▨	▨	▨	▨

cut my fly-fishing teeth. I still fish it more than any other river in the state with the possible exception in some years being the South Branch of the Raritan River.

The little black stonefly is the first good hatch to come off the Musconetcong River each year. And once these crazy fliers get going and the trout are on them they can make any hint of the winter blues go right out the window. Soon after that the Hendricksons show and the game really gets going, the trout are awake and looking up. Then comes the Grannom caddis, a slight lull with sparser hatches of various caddis and mayflies which is then followed by those beautiful little yellow mayflies we call pale evening duns or Sulphurs.

The sparser hatches I mentioned come in the way of March browns, blue-winged olives and the not-so-sparse-on-some-days cinnamon caddis. Take your pick or pick an attractor like an Adams or Royal Wulff, or one of my favorites, the Antbeetle. Either way you can have some pretty good dry-fly action more times than not from early spring to early summer.

By the time the pale evening duns come off the river it begins to switch gears and fishes best early and late in the day. Again, this is true of all New Jersey, and for that matter, all Eastern rivers and streams. Most notably the early morning Trico hatch on the Musky is excellent for a couple of weeks in June and into early July. You can also look for good midday action when the weather is cloudy and cool or cloudy and showery. These conditions bring out the blue-winged olives and the larger-than-average slate drakes, or *Isonychias*. Throughout this period count on late-day caddis hatches that vary in intensity from very light to moderate. Most are tan in color but you will also see some darker species. Either way, a well-placed imitation is more important than an exact imitation, just be observant and keep it close to what you see in the air or on the water.

South Branch of the Raritan River

(See river map on page 78)

Better known just as the "South Branch", this river starts out in Northern Morris County as a tiny freestone stream as it flows from Budd Lake through hills and farm country, this section of the river supports a healthy population of wild trout. Early in its travels, just above the town of Long Valley, a section known as the Claremont Stretch is maintained by the state as a trout conservation zone. This is the only Trout Conservation Area not stocked by the Division. It is a one-mile stretch of river in Long Valley that has naturally reproducing brook and brown trout. Here the river flows through high banks and is covered by a canopy of trees and streamside vegetation that keeps the water cool year round. This makes for excellent trout habitat but at the same time makes casting a challenge. But the reward of a properly placed cast and presentation is sometimes a beautifully speckled wild trout.

Further downstream near the town of Califon the river grows in volume and becomes more of a traditional trout stream with deep pools separated by riffles and pocket water. This water also sustains good numbers of stream-bred trout—mostly browns and brooks, but also some rainbows. It is also heavily stocked in spring and fall, offering the angler plenty of trout to cast a fly to.

Upper South Branch of the Raritan River.

About two miles downstream of the town of Califon the river flows into the Ken Lockwood Gorge. Here the river becomes very scenic as it runs for 2.5 miles between steep ridges lined with hardwoods and evergreens that hold large boulders in place on the mountainsides with their massive root systems, their thick canopies shading the river below. The river is mostly fast pocket water flowing noisily around many large and small boulders and deadfalls with some beautiful pools where the river levels off for brief periods. This is classic trout water that the state has designated a Year Round Trout Conservation Area where an angler may only keep one trout per day over 15 inches. Despite that, it seems most anglers practice catch-and-release fishing in the gorge, which helps it maintain a good hold-over population of nice-sized trout.

Although the gorge is stocked by the state, there is a good population of native stream-bred trout that hide in the shadows of the boulders and streamside trees. Just about any pool, run, pocket or riffle, no matter how wide or narrow, may hold a fish. I've taken fish in the gorge that were in water so skinny it barely covered their back. I

Photo by Mark Sagan

Ken Lockwood Gorge section South Branch of the Raritan River.

could not see them despite the clarity of the water, but they were there. Approach these stretches from below and whether you are fishing a dry fly or unweighted nymph, have confidence the fish are there, because they are. Just get a good, drag-free drift over the water and make sure your line falls well below your target so as not to scare them. It doesn't take much when they are in only a few inches of water, and they know a great blue heron patrols the area.

The gorge ends below the town of High Bridge and quickly goes from being primarily pocket water back to the more typical pool, riffle, pool trout stream. Just downstream of Clinton the river gains in size and widens offering the angler some excellent fly-fishing water from here all the way to the town of South Branch where it joins its little sister, the North Branch of the Raritan River. This stretch of water—from Clinton to South Branch—the river becomes a true coastal plain river as it meanders through some of New Jersey's most fertile farmland. There are long pools that change with every curve or bend imparted by the earth, rarely are both sides of the river of equal depth. Even the riffles will clearly show the angler where the fish should be and where he should wade. In some areas you will find mild pocket water broken by rocks and fueled by an increase in the gradient of the land. And finally, you will also find sharp, undercut banks lined with tall grasses or rows of corn in summer.

Photo by Mark Sagan

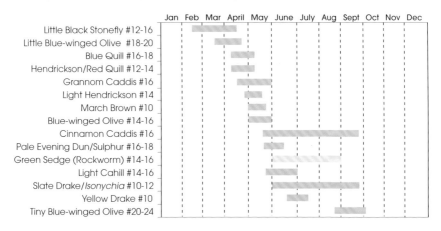

	Jan	Feb	Mar	April	May	June	July	Aug	Sept	Oct	Nov	Dec
Little Black Stonefly #12-16		▬▬▬	▬									
Little Blue-winged Olive #18-20			▬▬									
Blue Quill #16-18				▬▬								
Hendrickson/Red Quill #12-14				▬▬								
Grannom Caddis #16				▬▬▬								
Light Hendrickson #14				▬								
March Brown #10					▬▬							
Blue-winged Olive #14-16					▬							
Cinnamon Caddis #16						▬▬▬▬▬▬▬▬▬						
Pale Evening Dun/Sulphur #16-18						▬▬▬▬▬						
Green Sedge (Rockworm) #14-16						▬▬▬▬▬▬▬						
Light Cahill #14-16						▬▬▬▬						
Slate Drake/*Isonychia* #10-12						▬▬▬▬▬▬▬▬▬▬						
Yellow Drake #10						▬▬▬						
Tiny Blue-winged Olive #20-24									▬▬▬			

Although this section, from Clinton downstream, does have some decent mayfly hatches you are more likely to encounter caddis hatching on any given day or evening. The cinnamon caddis hatches almost daily from May to September, typically in the evenings into dusk. In late summer and into September you will find little dark smoky-colored caddis hatching and egg-laying. The trout will sip them in gently as though they are taking spinners. A size 18 dark gray spent-wing caddis works like a charm when these little fliers are on the water. In the summer months this stretch of water is also the perfect water for a well-placed hopper or beetle when nothing is hatching and the trout need to be coaxed into rising.

Throughout its length the South Branch has good hatches of mayflies, caddisflies, stoneflies and other aquatic insects the trout can feed on and which the angler can imitate with flies. The most prolific mayfly hatches are the Hendrickson, Sulphur, *Isonychia* and at different times of the year, blue-winged olives. In the chart above you'll note I have only listed a couple of caddisfly hatches, the reality is that there is at least one species of caddis every day from April through September on the river, usually more. Carry caddis patterns in the colors and sizes I suggest in the "Caddisflies" section (page 48) and you will be well prepared for most of the caddis hatches on the South Branch of the Raritan River. There are also good populations of baitfish, crayfish, and freshwater shrimp (scuds) to fatten hold-over fish,

turning some of them into real brutes. And as with all New Jersey rivers, the warmer months can bring excellent terrestrial fishing. Beautiful terrain, the gorge, plenty of trout and good access make the South Branch one of New Jersey's most popular trout waters.

Black River/ Lamington River

(See river map on page 79)

The Black River begins as a small trickle in Randolph Township just south of where Route 10 and Sussex Turnpike join. From here, the tiny stream flows for a mile or so through woods that separate it from nearby suburban neighborhoods before it enters the 3000-acre-plus Black River Wildlife Management Area (WMA) at Ironia Road in Randolph Township. Here the river spreads out and becomes part of a large marsh that's better suited to songbirds, ducks, and deer, than it is to trout. At varying points in the WMA the river is better defined than at others. In these stretches, there are some native trout along with state-reared trout that make their way up into this stretch from the Route 206 Bridge early in the season, which is the uppermost stocking point on the river. Once the summer comes though, there is little depth to the water and very few if any trout stick around to see how warm the water will get. The Black River WMA continues below Route 206 for another mile and a half or so to where it passes under Route 24. The river is still quite small here as it flows through relatively flat land, some of which again is quite marshy. It gets better defined the last half mile or so as it approaches Route 24.

Once the river passes under Route 24 in Chester it enters Black River County Park. Here its character changes dramatically as it now must wrestle the stubborn geology. While the river above here could meander slowly through marshy, even terrain, it now has to course through rocks and large boulders, over ledges and down steep crevasses. If you like fishing pocket water and small, tight pools where the river sings its bubbling songs as you do, this is the place for you. The clear, brisk water holds plenty of stocked and stream-bred trout.

About a half mile after the river enters the county park the land gives it brief respite as it flattens and slows the river some in places. This is just a breather for the both the angler and the river as the hard, steep earth will again take it under its control further south. The river is fished fairly heavily here throughout the spring season into early June. In summer, unless you fish it very early or late, you will be sharing the river with others who are more interested in joining the trout in the cool water than they are in catching them.

As the river continues through the County Park, the terrain is rocky and the river is shaded by hardwood trees and large hemlocks with roots that split the rocks and whose needles tint the water the color of tea. When the sun is high the bands of light pierce the canopy and dance on the water. You will catch both stocked and wild trout in the many pockets and runs topped with bubbles from beating against the hard remains of a glacial valley.

I like to fish the river here in the fall, working my way upstream with a Bead Head Pheasant Tail Nymph or Hare's Ear, making short, accurate casts directly upstream into the many small pockets and runs that course between the rocks and boulders. I usually manage to take a few fish this way, covering lots of water quickly while getting a good workout. It's one my favorite things to do on a cool, brisk autumn day when the sun is only at its best for a few hours.

Immediately after it leaves the County Park, the Black River enters a deep gorge that cuts through Hacklebarney State Park. Here the water cascades through a narrow glacial valley full of huge boulders and rocks that in places squeeze the river into a torrent of rushing white water, and in others forms majestic waterfalls. The river is

The Black River in Hacklebarney State Park.

Photo by NJ Dept. of Environmental Protection

The Lamington River in Bedminster.

Photo by Mark Sagan

the same river, same water, same watershed, but with a different name and appropriately, a different terrain. Before reaching this point, the river flowed through a rock-filled, glacial valley, shaded by hemlocks and from here it will meander lazily through relatively flat pastureland and stands of hardwoods before meeting up with the North Branch of the Raritan River. It is also important to note the Lamington River from where it "starts" on downstream to Lamington Road (Route 523) in Bedminster, the river flows through mostly private land.

From Lamington Road to the North Branch of the Raritan River the Lamington River is again stocked by the state. This stretch holds some stream-bred trout as well. The river here is a very typical New Jersey small stream, characterized by shallow riffles that slow as they spill into deeper, slower water forming nice, easy-to-fish pools. In between riffles and usually after a nice pool you will find plenty of deep, root-filled undercut banks to ply with a nymph or streamer when nothing is rising, or you might drift a big juicy terrestrial over just off the bank to a slow riser.

The Black River/Lamington River has a variety of hatches, but the most consistent are the caddisflies. The best mayfly hatches are the Sulphurs and blue-winged olives. Although none of the caddis of this river form blizzard hatches, they do hatch almost daily from April until September, and there are enough of them throughout the year to make fishing the larva or pupa productive. This is also a good river to fish terrestrials on during the warmer months.

loud and as you approach the river from above, you will hear it much sooner than you will see it. There are two main trails that lead down to the river from park headquarters and to the deepest parts of the gorge. These trails are the best way down to the river. Once down there, you can hike up or downstream to the more remote areas of the park. Like the County Park though, expect to see others along the way, especially in the warmest months of the year. But no matter what time of the year you visit Hacklebarney State Park, expect to be taken in by all the natural beauty that will surround you.

At the lower end of Hacklebarney State Park the Black River enters the Black River Fish and Game Club, which is private. The state does not stock below the park for this reason and from the club into the town of Pottersville there is no public access to the river.

Oh, and Pottersville is also notable because somewhere, somehow in this tiny hamlet the Black River becomes the Lamington River. It is

Black/Lamington River Primary Hatches

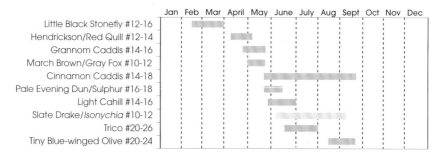

	Jan	Feb	Mar	April	May	June	July	Aug	Sept	Oct	Nov	Dec
Little Black Stonefly #12-16		▓	▓									
Hendrickson/Red Quill #12-14			▓									
Grannom Caddis #14-16				▓								
March Brown/Gray Fox #10-12				▓								
Cinnamon Caddis #14-18					▓	▓	▓	▓	▓			
Pale Evening Dun/Sulphur #16-18						▓						
Light Cahill #14-16						▓	▓					
Slate Drake/*Isonychia* #10-12						▓	▓	▓	▓			
Trico #20-26							▓	▓				
Tiny Blue-winged Olive #20-24									▓			

North Branch of the Raritan River.

North Branch of the Raritan River

(See river map on page 80)

The North Branch of the Raritan River, the "North Branch", begins just a few miles east of the Black River/Lamington River in Northwest Morris County and follows a similar north to south route a safe distance to the east before the Lamington turns east to join it just south of Route 78 in Bedminster. From here the North Branch continues south until it joins the South Branch of the Raritan River in Somerset County.

The Division of Fish and Game stocks the North Branch from Peapack Road Bridge in Far Hills down to its confluence with the South Branch, about twelve miles of water. Above Peapack Road most of the river flows through estates and private property where access is limited. So we will concentrate only on the water that is accessible to the public, and there is plenty of it.

The North Branch is a fairly small, freestone river where it passes through Far Hills and Bedminster. It has high banks that are lined by hardwood trees and low-growing shrubs that provide shade for the river and it inhabitants and headaches for those who ignore the path of their back cast. The river bed is rock-strewn with lots of good holding water that varies from slow, deep pools to quick riffles and runs.

As the river flows further south it passes under Route 202/206 in Bedminster where it increases in size and depth. Here the river is paralleled by River Road East for about two miles, which provides access to some nice water that fishes best in the spring and fall months. There are some deep pools here and long undercut banks that hold fish throughout the year. There are also several islands that separate the river in this stretch.

After the river passes under Route 78 it flows a short ways before it crosses under Burnt Mills Road and is joined by the Lamington River. Here it meanders through farmland for about four miles where access is limited before reaching North Branch Park in Bridgewater. The park offers easy access to about a mile of river and access to another mile below before the North Branch joins the South Branch to become the Raritan River. This section tends to get quite warm in the summer and so it is more of a seasonal trout stream here relying on stocking to maintain its trout population.

North Branch of the Raritan River Primary Hatches

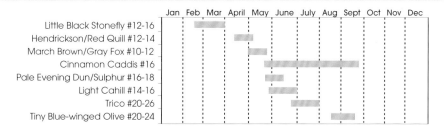

	Jan	Feb	Mar	April	May	June	July	Aug	Sept	Oct	Nov	Dec
Little Black Stonefly #12-16		■	■									
Hendrickson/Red Quill #12-14				■								
March Brown/Gray Fox #10-12					■	■						
Cinnamon Caddis #16						■	■	■	■			
Pale Evening Dun/Sulphur #16-18					■	■						
Light Cahill #14-16						■	■					
Trico #20-26							■	■				
Tiny Blue-winged Olive #20-24									■	■		

Passaic River in Chatham.

Passaic River
(See river map on page 81)

Depending on where you live in New Jersey you may think of the Passaic River as a turbid, over-industrialized, flood-prone river, or a small, crystal-clear brook flowing through swampy hardwood stands echoing with the music of songbirds. And those are just two of the many faces of this river that flows for ninety miles through 45 cities and towns, over two dams, and in between them, the Great Falls in Paterson. The Passaic River is also living proof that conscientious environmental legislation and hard-working coalitions can and do make a difference in the restoration of a river. The work is not done, but in the short span of my lifetime I have seen many positive changes in the river that as a kid was the subject of jokes.

The trout fisherman need only be concerned with the upper thirty miles of the Passaic River as the lower two-thirds hold only warmwater species. And even in this upper section it needs to be broken down into sections as there are some stretches of the river that are too slow and silted to hold trout.

I'll start with the uppermost section of the Passaic from its source to where it enters the

Great Swamp National Wildlife Refuge. This section of the river is quite small and mostly pocket water, riffles and small pools. Much of the surrounding terrain is swampy and filled with tall, majestic hardwood trees that are home to dozens of songbirds. This section of the river is not stocked by the Division of Fish and Wildlife as it is designated a Wild Trout Stream in this area. A portion of the stream here flows through the New Jersey Audubon Society's Scherman-Hoffman Wildlife Sanctuary. If you want to fish their property, you must go to the center and get a special permit first. The banks of the river are environmentally sensitive so be careful when walking the banks of the river. The rule here is: "Leave only footprints and take only photos and memories." I would go so far as to say this rule applies anywhere you fish, although where permitted keep a few for the grill if your tastes include fresh trout. Also, the river is protected where it flows through the Great Swamp and therefore, no fishing is permitted within the Refuge.

After the Passaic River leaves the Great Swamp it flows through Basking Ridge and southward to Millington. From White Bridge Road

	Jan	Feb	Mar	April	May	June	July	Aug	Sept	Oct	Nov	Dec
Little Black Stonefly #12-16		▓	▓									
Hendrickson/Red Quill #12-14				▓								
Grannom Caddis #16					▓							
Cinnamon Caddis #16						▓	▓	▓	▓			
Pale Evening Dun/Sulphur #16-18					▓	▓						
Light Cahill #14-16					▓	▓						

to Valley Road in Millington, a distance of just over three river miles, the Division of Fish and Wildlife stocks the river with trout in both the spring and fall months. Here the river varies from short riffles, runs and small pools to large, fairly deep pools. The average width of the river is about 20-25 feet. A lot of the river here is accessible, but like most of our rivers, if you are willing to walk a few hundred yards from an access you can have the river all to yourself.

From Valley Road in Millington to Chatham the river flows over land that has little gradient causing it to move slowly for most of the year. This condition has created a silty bottom and a tendency for the water to warm far too much to support trout. Here the river holds bass, carp and catfish, but few trout.

I grew up in Chatham a few blocks up the hill from the Passaic River where it forms the border between Chatham and Summit. When I was a kid we used to fish the river regularly here for catfish and carp and the occasional largemouth bass. The river then was fairly turbid much of the time and silted in many sections. During the warmer months of the year algae and long water grasses would dance with the current in the shallower stretches, the carp holding tight under the moving shadow. We fished the Passaic from April to October, mostly catching carp on our special homemade cornmeal-dough concoction heavily laced with vanilla flavoring, some of them quite large and full of piss and vinegar when hooked. As I got older we used fly rods and flies that imitated mulberries or Woolly Worms to catch these giant golden minnows known as freshwater bonefish to some for good reason. Never did I imagine that when I reached the time of my life when my children were entering college, the same stretches of water we once tossed worms and cornmeal balls wrapped around hooks into would be stocked with trout.

Now this border stretch has changed considerably in recent years thanks to changes in how surrounding towns, industries and the public utilize the river. So much so that the New Jersey Division of Fish and Wildlife began stocking the river with trout from the Mount Vernon Road bridge in Chatham Township to the Route 24 bridge in Chatham Borough, a distance of about two miles. Much of this stretch is protected and accessible as the land bordering the river has been designated Passaic River Park. Although Chatham and Summit both have nearby neighborhoods, much of the river here has wooded banks that shade the river well and offer the angler solitude.

As the Passaic River recovers in this stretch so does the insect life living on and in the water. There are decent caddis hatches that will bring the trout up to the surface to feed, as well some of the hardier mayfly species. I have seen noticeable increases in the numbers of both types of insects as the years go by. There are also good numbers of scuds in the river here, as well as crayfish and minnows.

Rockaway River
(See river map on page 82)

The Rockaway River flows through secluded woodlands, residential neighborhoods, commercial and industrial zones, and everything in between. For most of the 20th Century the commercial and industrial interests bordering the river had the upper hand and the rivers condition was in a sharp decline. But fortunately over the last 20 years or so this has changed a great deal thanks to the successful restoration efforts of several dedicated organizations and positive changes in environmental legislation.

The river begins as the outflow of a small lake in Sussex County where it flows for a short distance through forested lands before entering Northwest Morris County. Here it meanders into and out of a

New Jersey Rivers

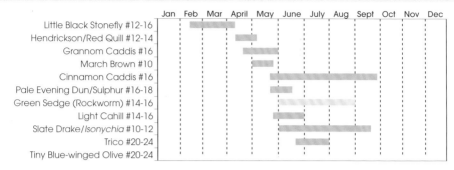

	Jan	Feb	Mar	April	May	June	July	Aug	Sept	Oct	Nov	Dec
Little Black Stonefly #12-16		■	■									
Hendrickson/Red Quill #12-14				■								
Grannom Caddis #16				■	■							
March Brown #10					■							
Cinnamon Caddis #16						■	■	■	■	■		
Pale Evening Dun/Sulphur #16-18						■						
Green Sedge (Rockworm) #14-16						■	■	■				
Light Cahill #14-16						■	■	■				
Slate Drake/*Isonychia* #10-12						■	■	■	■	■		
Trico #20-24							■	■	■			
Tiny Blue-winged Olive #20-24												

The Rockaway River meanders through a quiet autumn day.

Photo by Jason Kurtz

group of ponds and lakes before it enters shallow Oak Ridge Lake. After leaving Oak Ridge Lake it flows only a short distance before it fills Longwood Lake in Jefferson Township. The Division of Fish and Game begins stocking the river where it exits the dam below Longwood Lake.

From Longwood Lake south to Route 15, a distance of about 5 miles, Berkshire Valley Road runs parallel to the river giving the angler good access. Here the Rockaway twists and turns its way through the valley bordered mostly by thick hardwood stands growing on steep, rocky inclines. Here the river is a combination of pocket water, swift runs and large and small pools that hold good numbers of trout throughout the year.

The Rockaway River moves into Wharton shortly after it flows under Route 80 and takes a turn eastward. This is the first of many towns it will flow through on its journey to the Passaic River. From Wharton it makes its way to Dover where it moves through the remnants of the industrial age, a channel that confines it as it moves through the town and then alongside railroad tracks. Here the river remains clear despite being surrounded by streets, yards and buildings just a stone's throw away through the sparse trees that line the river bank.

After the river leaves Dover it again flows unrestricted through rocky, tree-lined banks as it flows northeast towards Rockaway, Denville, and finally Boonton before emptying in the Jersey City Reservoir. Throughout this twelve-mile stretch the river flows through secluded wooded areas, parks, golf courses, suburban neighborhoods, commercial zones and over a couple of dams that slow and widen the river. Just before it reaches the reservoir it cascades down through a rock-filled gorge. The river's character varies as it winds its way through these towns. In some stretches it has the classic trout water look of deep pools separated by long and short riffles and runs, to pocket water, to slow lazy pools. Access in this stretch is good via many nearby roads, crossroads (bridges) and parks.

The Rockaway River has some fairly good hatches of mayflies, caddisflies and other aquatic insects that continue to improve each year with the river's condition. It also has a good population of one of the trout's favorite foods, scuds. In some sections they are so prevalent that you can grab a bunch of aquatic grass in your hand and it will appear to be alive there are so many scuds moving around in it.

Pequannock River
(See river map on page 83)

The Pequannock River may be New Jersey's most unique trout stream as the majority of it flows through protected lands owned by the City of Newark. This status has served to break the river

Pequannock River Wild Trout Area.

up into a couple of sections that are separated by large reservoirs. Its headwaters are found in northeastern Sussex County, where it flows south into Oak Ridge Reservoir. Above the reservoir fishing is not permitted, so its trout fishing potential is not realized until it flows out of Oak Ridge Reservoir. It is also unique because all of the brown trout in it are wild fish.

Below Oak Ridge Reservoir the Pequannock is a true tailwater fishery that flows for about five miles before it enters Charlottesburg Reservoir. This entire section of river is classified as a "Wild Trout Stream" as it supports a healthy population of wild brown and brook trout, with the former being by far the most prevalent. Here the river flows clear and cool over a rocky, boulder-strewn bottom shaded on both sides by large evergreens and hardwood trees. There is very little broken water through this entire stretch and the flow is very consistent bank to bank and quite deep in some places.

Thankfully, the watershed commission has successfully regulated flows in this section making it ideal habitat for brown trout

Pequannock River Primary Hatches

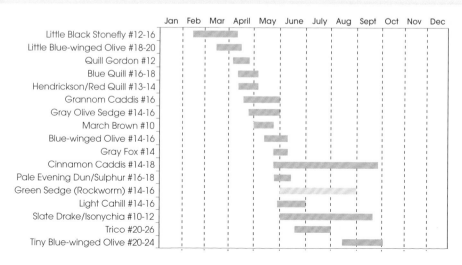

Hatch	Jan	Feb	Mar	April	May	June	July	Aug	Sept	Oct	Nov	Dec
Little Black Stonefly #12-16		▓	▓									
Little Blue-winged Olive #18-20			▓									
Quill Gordon #12				▓								
Blue Quill #16-18				▓								
Hendrickson/Red Quill #13-14				▓								
Grannom Caddis #16					▓							
Gray Olive Sedge #14-16					▓							
March Brown #10					▓							
Blue-winged Olive #14-16					▓							
Gray Fox #14					▓							
Cinnamon Caddis #14-18						▓	▓	▓	▓			
Pale Evening Dun/Sulphur #16-18						▓	▓					
Green Sedge (Rockworm) #14-16						▓	▓	▓				
Light Cahill #14-16						▓	▓					
Slate Drake/Isonychia #10-12						▓	▓	▓				
Trico #20-26							▓	▓				
Tiny Blue-winged Olive #20-24								▓	▓			

reproduction. And these are special browns not only because they are stream-bred fish, but because they exhibit all the tendencies for which brown trout are famous. They are wily, stream-smart fish that are prone to only feeding on top when there is a bonafide mayfly or caddisfly hatch—blind fishing a dry fly is often a waste of one's time except in the summer months when terrestrials abound. This is not to say that the Pequannock River between the reservoirs has limited aquatic insect life. In fact, it has some great hatches of both mayflies and caddisflies throughout the season.

Also, because the brown trout here feed on the abundant minnows and crayfish they share the river with, they can grow quite large. Actually, regardless of their size, the fish in this section are accustomed to feeding on fairly large food items as, in addition to the aforementioned items, there is also a thriving population of hellgrammite and cranefly larvae crawling among the subsurface rocks. For these reasons, always be prepared to fish with nymphs or streamers, and make sure you fish some that are on the large size. In order to fish this section of the Pequannock, you must first obtain a permit from the Newark Watershed Conservation & Development Corporation. The office is located on Echo Lake Road of Route 23, in Newfoundland.

After the Pequannock River leaves Charlottesburg Reservoir fishing is not permitted until the river reaches the Route 23 Bridge at Smoke Rise. Here the river is classified as a Seasonal Trout Conservation Area for a distance of about 1.2 miles downstream to the Route 23 bridge at Smith Mills. A permit is NOT required to fish the Seasonal TCA. Like the Wild Trout Stream water above the reservoir this section is restricted to the use of artificial lures only and bait of any kind is prohibited. There are good hatches here and access is fairly easy as Route 23 parallels the river from bridge to bridge. And unlike the Wild Trout Section, this part of the river is stocked by the Division of Fish and Wildlife, but only with brook and rainbow trout.

Before moving on down the rest of the Pequannock I would like to stress something about this river that applies throughout its trout-fishing length. The river bed for the most part is made up of rocks and boulders of varying sizes that are very slippery, making for dangerous wading. I recommend fishing it using studded, felt-soled wading shoes or cleats and a wading staff. Don't wait until you fall on your ass and break something before doing this as many others before have.

Downstream of Smith Mills there are approximately five more miles of river that offer the fly-fisherman quality trout fishing where general trout-fishing regulations apply. Here the river continues to be lined with hardwood trees as it flows through the towns of Butler, Bloomingdale, Riverdale and finally Pompton Lakes. And although most of the landscape is suburban, the Pequannock still offers excellent trout-fishing year round for stocked and hold-over rainbow and brook trout, as well as wild browns. Hatches are good here and gaining access to the river is also not much of a problem.

Ramapo River

(See river map on page 84)

The Ramapo River begins its journey south in New York State, where it collects 110 square miles of its total drainage of 160 square miles. It enters

Ramapo River.

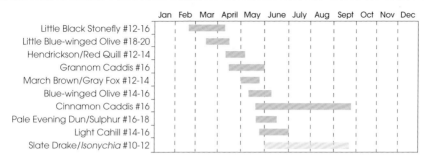

	Jan	Feb	Mar	April	May	June	July	Aug	Sept	Oct	Nov	Dec
Little Black Stonefly #12-16		▨	▨									
Little Blue-winged Olive #18-20			▨	▨								
Hendrickson/Red Quill #12-14				▨								
Grannom Caddis #16				▨	▨							
March Brown/Gray Fox #12-14					▨							
Blue-winged Olive #14-16					▨							
Cinnamon Caddis #16						▨	▨	▨	▨			
Pale Evening Dun/Sulphur #16-18					▨							
Light Cahill #14-16					▨	▨						
Slate Drake/*Isonychia* #10-12					▨	▨	▨	▨	▨			

New Jersey in Bergen County, where it collects the other 50 square miles of its drainage and only flows for a mere 10 miles or so before reaching Pompton Lake. It is also a stone's throw from New York City and well within the Tri-State Metropolitan Area where the world moves at its fastest pace. Nevertheless, the Ramapo has a solid following of fly-anglers who know they can step into its nerve-calming, tree-lined waters and forget about the rat race that buzzes just a short train ride away.

The Ramapo is an angler-friendly river that flows through a varied landscape of suburban residential areas, wooded glens, ball fields and the

occasional commercial landscapes. Fortunately, much of the immediately adjacent river-bank areas are mostly wooded. The river is stocked by the state with ample numbers of trout in both the spring and fall, and many of these fish hold-over from season to season, affording the angler year-round opportunities to fish for trout. Access is fairly easy as Route 202 parallels the east side of the river for most of its length. The character of the river is as varied as the terrain it flows through the pocket water, riffles, runs, pools, and some areas that are deep, slow and more like a lake than a river. One of these sections is large enough to be called Potash Lake. Because of these slower areas some sections of the stream do warm up in the summer months. During these times the trout will congregate in the cooler, swifter sections of the river or in the depths of the slow, lake-like sections.

Hatches on the Ramapo are limited to some extent due to siltation, but there are more than enough other aquatic life forms for the fly-fisher to imitate. The best mayfly hatches on the river are the pale evening duns (Sulphurs), blue-winged olives, and *Isonychias* (slate-winged drakes). Various caddis species hatch from April to October with the cinnamon caddis being the most prolific. The Ramapo also has midge hatches throughout the year.

The faster sections of the Ramapo – the riffles and pocket water – hold decent numbers of *Isonychia* mayfly nymphs. I have had some very good days fishing the Ramapo with nymphs and wet flies that mimic the large, slender *Isonychia* nymphs that hatch sporadically from late June through September. In particular, I like

New Jersey Rivers

to dead-drift and/or swing a Leadwing Coachman wet fly in the pocket water around boulders and rocks and in the faster sections of the river that this mayfly prefers. The primary material in the Leadwing Coachman wet fly is peacock herl and so any peacock-herl-bodied nymph or wet fly will do. Traditional patterns with peacock herl, such as the Zug Bug and Prince Nymph in sizes #10-12, will work just fine.

The Ramapo River has one other aquatic inhabitant worth noting—the scud. The river has a healthy population of scuds throughout its length and the trout become accustomed to feeding on them shortly after they enter the river.

Lastly, like all New Jersey rivers terrestrials such as ants and beetles offer the dry-fly angler good fishing early and late in the day from June right into September.

Toms River

(See river map on page 85)

Toms River flows through the northern part of one of the nation's most ecologically diverse regions east of the Mississippi River, known as the Pine Barrens. The Toms is one of a few trout streams in the "southern" half of New Jersey, and the only one with a Year Round Trout Conservation Area. Typical of an Eastern coastal-plain river, the Toms is unhurried as it flows in a continuous series of

Toms River Bonefish Darter.

"S" curves throughout much of its length above the tidal zone. Its tea-colored water is also characteristic of a river flowing through these regions, as the rains filtering through accumulated decaying organic matter on the sandy soil it flows through leaches into them. In periods when rain is scarce, the river becomes crystal clear and its trout very wary, preferring to hide in the shelter of the many undercut, brush-laden banks.

The uppermost section of the Toms is a narrow, tightly winding stream surrounded by mostly deciduous trees and thick brush. Access here is relatively good with many nearby roads. Because the river is small here and the banks full of growth, wading must be done with caution. It is best done by working your way upstream with a short rod and quick, accurate casts. You do not

Toms River.

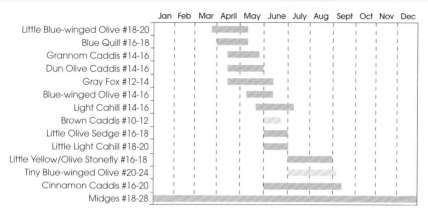

want to give the trout any time to feel your presence. The state stocks ample numbers of trout in both the spring and fall months in this section—the Route 528 Bridge to where the Maple Root branch enters the river. There is also a good population of small, stream-bred brook trout here.

Beginning in the lower end of the upper stocked section of the Toms, the river begins to widen and the hardwood trees are replaced by stands of pines, cedars, and holly trees. The surrounding land becomes swampy and canoe hatches are a daily occurrence in the warmer months of the year. The best times to fish this section are early morning or late in the day, especially from late May through September.

From where the Maple Root Branch enters the Toms to the Route 70 Bridge, access to the river is difficult, especially on foot. But if you are intrepid and want solitude and a beautiful environment to fish in, this is the place for you. The river here is alternately bordered by swampy areas full of high grasses and stands of pine trees, holly and other conifers that the sun must force its way through in thin bands of light that shimmer and glow. This is the Pine Barrens in all its glory; scenic and echoing with the songs of the multitude of birds that call this land home and others there for a rest before heading north or south depending on the season. Although the river is not stocked here, there is a healthy population of stream-bred trout, as well as some stocked trout that migrate from above and below.

Much of the lower section of the Toms, from the Route 70 Bridge down to where it passes under Route 571, the river has good access via Riverwood Park. The state also stocks this section of the river in both the spring and fall months. The last mile or so of this section, from the park border to Route 571, is a year-round Trout Conservation Area.

The biology of the Toms is such that it sustains only a very limited number of mayfly species, yet has excellent habitat for many caddisfly species. It also supports a wide variety of small Chironomids—"midges"—throughout the year. In the warmer months, some days all you will need are a few ants and beetles to catch fish. And lastly, it supports a healthy population of tessellated darters—small, amber-colored minnows with distinct dark-brown mottling on their back and sides and large-ringed eyes. A well-respected trout bum I know imitates the darter with a tan bonefish fly and does quite well with it on the Toms.

Wild Trout Streams

Despite being one of the smallest, most densely populated states in the country, New Jersey has many wild trout streams. In all, there are about 175 streams that support populations of wild trout. Of these, there are 35 that have been designated Wild Trout Streams by the NJ Division of Fish and Wildlife. These rivers are protected by special state fishing regulations and they do not get stocked. Be sure to check the NJ Division of

New Jersey Rivers

NJ trout stream in autumn.

Fish and Wildlife Fishing Regulations booklet before you go as the regulations may change from year to year. This booklet also lists the designated 35 Wild Trout Streams.

Most of the Wild Trout Streams are fairly small, clear brooks that tumble over rocks and boulders and fall into pools formed by years of flowing water. Some are found in the mountainous northwestern part of the state and are surrounded by stands of hemlock and hardwoods. Others wander through farmland and are only a stone's throw away from residential developments. Some of these rivers have just one species of trout inhabiting them and others may have two, and there only three that have all three species: brook, brown and rainbow trout. Brook trout are the most common for good reason; they are native to New Jersey.

The one thing all of New Jersey's Wild Trout streams have in common is the fish. Although they

The Big Flatbrook River as seen through the trees.

are on the small side, they make up for it with their vivid coloring, bright spots and translucent fins. Every one is a rare jewel unto itself that glows with Nature's beauty. Add to this the fact that every one of these wild trout seems to possess a spirited disposition; when hooked they leap and jump like school kids on a trampoline for the first time. Simply put, every one is beautiful.

Because I believe this resource is so valuable, I am going to make some recommendations for those of you who fish the Wild Trout Streams. Please use barbless hooks, and when you land one bring it close without taking it out of the water and grabbing the fly in its jaw. Take in its colors and energy, and then back the hook out and watch it swim away. If you must handle it, wet your hand first and cradle it gently without squeezing. After you take a picture of it, get it back in the water quickly.

Other New Jersey Trout Streams

In addition to the previously mentioned rivers and streams, New Jersey has dozens of other trout streams that have stocked and/or wild fish in them. Some of these streams are somewhat remote, some meander through Wildlife Management Areas, and others separate one suburban neighborhood from

Photo by Jessica Lettich

another. No matter where they are though, all of these rivers have something to offer the fly-fisherman. It could be as simple as the river being near where you live, and therefore, you can hit it after work on the way home. Other streams may be worth your while just for the sake of exploring new water. You may even find one that over time becomes that special river where the solitude you find there is just as important to you as the fishing.

One of the nice things about exploring these rivers and streams is that they are like a box of chocolates: you never know what you are going to get. You might hook into a standard-issue brown or rainbow, or it may be a beautiful, brightly colored, six-inch-long wild brook trout. You may also cast your fly into a deep pool that's barely larger than a bathtub and pull out a 20-inch, five-pound rainbow. Either way you will be better for it as you can never fish too many different streams in your lifetime and every one will teach you something you didn't know before you wet your line in it.

The rivers listed in this chapter are the larger, more popular rivers and streams. Most of the other waters average about 15-20 feet across. Some are much smaller, maybe five or six feet on average, and others are slightly larger. Depending on the watershed, some of these streams will become very high and off-color when it rains because they are in more suburban areas where there is a lot of runoff from streets and storm sewers. Others that are away from suburbia and flow through wooded areas and undeveloped land may come up also when it rains, but not as much, and they tend to recover much faster.

There are many small rivers in New Jersey that in their lower reaches flow through towns, but if you go up stream where the roads thin out you can find some great water. There are many streams like this that support trout all year long and some that even have wild trout in them. The key to fishing these streams is to walk up- or downstream from the access to find good water. If you do fish only near the access point—a bridge or road alongside the stream—you will not get any solitude unless it is the dead of winter. You will also find that many of these smaller steams will offer you the challenges that you seek simply because they are new and different than the more popular rivers. You should

*Another beautiful New Jersey native brook trout taken from
a small Sussex County Wild Trout Stream.*

also know there are many small streams in the state that are wild-trout streams in the upper reaches but the lower reaches are primarily supported by the stocking of trout. The Passaic River is a good example of one.

You still have to fish these streams just like the larger ones, and maybe even more carefully because there is less room for error. Before entering a pool or run you have to size it up and figure out where the trout-holding water is and where the best place to wade is, so as not to spook the trout. Sometimes this means not wading at all, instead you have to hug the bank and cast sidearm over the water, and/or you may even have to crawl along the bank and cast from your knees. But it is all worth it when you see your line twitch because a trout took your nymph or your dry fly disappears from the surface into the mouth of a vividly colored wild brook trout.

I have a friend who a few years ago decided in January that he was going to fish all of the designated wild-trout streams in New Jersey and catch a trout from each. He did it by the middle of the summer that year. So, then he figured he would spend the rest of the year fishing all of the other trout streams that were not on the weekly spring stocking schedule. He fished a couple times a week through the rest of the year and fished dozens of streams. He wound up enjoying the challenge so much that he did the same thing the next year, except after he had fished the wild-trout streams, he only fished the smaller trout streams that he had not the year before. He swears those two years were the two in which he learned the most about fly-fishing. The third year he fished less and stuck close to home, he had to save his marriage.

Now the big questions becomes, what hatches do these streams have and what do you use when there is nothing hatching. We will start with what to use when there is no hatch. Simple, use the flies you have the most confidence in. You will fish them properly and they will catch fish because you know they work for you. If you are just starting out, go with those patterns I have listed in the fly-patterns chapter, or check with one of the fly shops in the state. As for hatches, most of these streams have the hatches you will read about in the next few chapters, only they will be lighter in most cases. Some of these streams will have good hatches of some insects and few of others. That's part of the fun of fly-fishing—every trip is a new learning experience.

A Warren County trout stream in early spring, Hendrickson time.

A male Hendrickson dun, one of New Jersey's best mayfly hatches year in and year out.

New Jersey Hatches

Mayflies

Mayfly hatches will always be my favorite to fish no matter what trout stream I am on. There is something about the way the adults appear like magic on the surface of a stream as they hatch out of their nymphal shucks just below the water surface. Some come out fully formed—wings upright, tails splayed—while others appear with their wings still folded on their thoraxes. These flies drift along and you can watch as they fill their wings with the fluids of life. The wings unfold and extend to full shape like a balloon being blown up. Once the wings are fully formed, the insects drift like tiny sailboats until they gain the strength to take flight and leave their formerly watery world into the atmosphere.

Now not all of them are as fortunate as others, many disappear from the water surface in a bubble, a gulp, or sip from a trout below getting its daily sustenance. And that of course is what we fly-fishermen are looking for. Once you see a trout take an adult, you fix the location in your mind's eye against a marker—a log, tree, rock or other fixed object. You think, OK, it's taking flies about ten feet off the opposite bank straight out from that reddish boulder.

Your senses heighten and you crouch a little and begin false casting bent forward towards your target. On the end of your tippet is a size-16 Catskill-style Hendrickson dry fly. As you false cast, the fish rises to take another natural; you note it's still in the same location. Once you think you have enough line out so you can drop your fly two to three feet above the fish, you make one last back cast and then quickly turn over your rod and point the tip at your target. The line gently unfurls on the water and the leader and tippet extend in an "S" with the fly landing a short distance above where the trout rose. You watch with relaxed tension and whisper pleading to the fish, Take it…perfect…come on.

Your fly drifts with the current down over the bull's-eye and then disappears into a small vortex that sends concentric rings on the water surface out from the center. At the same time you hear a soft SIP. You lift the rod tip and with your right arm, tighten the line in your left hand to set the hook firmly in the trout's jaw. Fish on!

There are three life-cycle stages of the mayfly an angler needs to be aware of in order to be a successful fly-fisherman. Four if you count emergers; so four it is, I do count them and you should too. They are the nymph, the emerger, the adult (subimago), and the spinner (imago). We will use adult and spinner for clarity, as that is what the artificial flies are mostly referred to as. The adult is the immature stage, and the spinner is the sexually mature stage: more on this later.

Mayfly Nymphs – We know that trout feed under the surface over 80% of their lives. That's because that is where the food is most of the time. In the case of mayflies, it is the nymphs that live on the bottom under rocks and stones, burrowed into sandy bottoms, and in plant matter. This is the larval stage of the mayfly, just like a caterpillar is to a butterfly.

Mayflies live as nymphs for roughly 365 days before they hatch, give or take a few days depending on the weather and water temperature. This means they are present for most of the year and therefore, the trout feed on them all year long, as they don't all hatch at the same time.

Because they live in a dynamic ever-changing environment, nymphs are always getting dislodged and swept downstream. When this happens they are fair game for the trout as they tumble and twist in the current trying to get back to the safety of the stream bottom. Nymphs also intentionally move into the water column when they are ready to hatch.

When it is time for the nymph to hatch, depending on the genus, some will swim to the surface and then break open the dorsal side of their nymphal shuck before climbing out as a winged adult on the water surface. Others will break through their nymphal shuck while still clinging to the bottom before swimming to the surface with their wings ready to go. When the insects get to the surface, they fill their wings with liquid life and once they are fully formed, fly away.

The bottom line here is that fishing nymphs is a very effective way to catch trout. It is different than fishing a dry fly as you cannot see the fly as it drifts and tumbles under the surface. It also takes more concentration to be consistently successful because you have to "feel" the way the fly is drifting and know how to maneuver your rod and line to prevent the fly from dragging unnaturally. Because they have three or four body shapes you do not need a different nymph for each mayfly species. Instead you can have a few different kinds in a few colors and sizes and do quite well with them.

Mayfly Emergers – Perhaps the most effective stage of the mayfly to imitate during a hatch is the emerger. This is because they are at their most vulnerable and somehow the trout know it. It makes sense when you think about it – the adult is fully formed but still trapped in the nymphal shuck struggling to free itself as it drifts towards and then under the surface; or the adult has left its shell on the bottom and is swimming to the surface with its wings exposed and catching the current. It should be noted that there are some mayfly species that hatch on the bottom, but instead of swimming to the surface, they crawl out on submerged rocks or vegetation before drying their wings and flying away.

You want to have some fun? Fish an emerger just before and/or during a hatch. As the mature nymphs become active in the morning and begin swimming and making false ascents to the surface, you'll see trout flashing and darting under the surface chasing these nymphs. The daylight that enters the water revealing them as it reflects off their sides when they dart and turn to take the hapless insects. You tie on a wet fly or subsurface emerger and swing it through the area you see the activity. Whether the trout take your fly on the dead-drift or on the swing as it rises to the surface from the tightening of the line below you, they take it hard. Your line suddenly darts, or shifts, or just jumps away from you. You can't miss it and if you strike too hard, you'll break the fish off.

As the day progresses, you begin to see some emerging flies on the surface. The trout start to break the surface as they chase the flies, gulping and slashing the half-emerged helpless flies. You change flies to a surface emerger and your fly barely hits the water before it gets ripped under by a winter-hungry trout. Lift your rod and he's on. It's some very exciting fishing.

Mayfly Adults – Depending on the atmospheric conditions and the mood of the trout, sometimes you can stay with the emerger right through the hatch and continue to catch fish. Other times you will notice, the trout will only take a fully emerged adult as it dries its wings in preparation of flight—now is the time to tie an adult imitation on the end of your tippet.

The fishing continues to be fun because you can see your cast land on the water and gauge how your fly is floating in relation to the current. You can mend your line or just pick up your fly and cast again if you don't like what you see. This is critical when fishing dry flies as the fly must float "drag-free"—as though it is not attached to anything. If the tippet is too heavy for the size of the fly or it is just too stiff or curled, the fly will move unnaturally—it gets pulled a tiny fraction of an inch in a different direction or speed than the current on which it is floating. The trout can detect this instantly and will not take the fly.

Sometimes I like to stop fishing and just observe when adult mayflies blanket the surface of the water. You pick a smooth section of water to concentrate your gaze and watch the tiny sailboat-like flies. Some suddenly take flight, while others, barely dry, get sipped in from below. As you watch you will notice they are all different as some will appear and instantly fly off, while others will drift, spastically flapping their wings as though they must test them to see if they are worthy of flight. If they find their wings are suitable, they will soon take off if they are fortunate enough to escape the trout's eager jaws.

Mayfly Spinners – What happens to the adult mayflies that manage to fly off into the streamside vegetation is nothing short of miraculous. Depending on the species, some will molt in a few hours, others over night, while still others will take a day or two. When they do molt they go from having satiny wings and dull bodies to clear-winged, glossy-bodied insects. Some will have tails that are now more than twice the length of their bodies.

Photo by Dennis Cabarle

Mayfly – Hendrickson spinner.

When these now-mature insects leave the safety of the brush and head out over the river it is a sight to see. Some species will do this at dusk, others at dawn, and still others midday if conditions permit. They will congregate over a specific water type depending on the species—some over riffles, some over smooth glides and still others over calm pools. They will dance up and down forming living clouds anywhere from several feet above the water to 20 and even 30 feet. Again, this will depend on the species. They dance to attract the opposite sex. Many times you will see the females with their bright yellow, orange or green egg sacs weighing down the end of their abdomens.

Once the spinners have mated, they fall spent to the water and release their eggs to drift to the bottom. The now-dying spinners drift feebly in the surface film making for an easy meal for the trout. You will know when trout are taking spinners—it's a soft blip or sip followed by the telltale concentric outward-moving rings—there is no need for the fish to expend energy eating them, they are not going anywhere. Sometimes the water surface will be blanketed with the sprawled-out spinners, making it difficult for the trout to pick your fly out from the naturals. When this happens, I usually tie on an attractor such as a Royal Wulff, it will stand out to me and the fish. It doesn't always work, but when your spinner is just one of thousands, it does give you hope being able to tell your fly from the others on the water.

Mayfly Hatches – The following are the common names of the more important mayflies that hatch in New Jersey, along with their distribution, size, hatch calendar, descriptions for identifying the adult, and lastly, the most useful imitation stage during a hatch period.

───────── Distribution Key ─────────
Widespread – Hatches in good numbers from most waters and very well on some of the larger rivers and streams. Rare on some waters.
Common – Hatches on most waters and depending on the location and quality of water the number of insects will vary from moderate to very light. May not be found on some waters.
Limited – Hatches in good numbers only on select waters and very sparsely on others. Not found at all on some.
Infrequent – Rarely found hatching in decent numbers where they do occur and not at all on many streams.

LITTLE BLUE-WINGED OLIVE – COMMON
#18-20; Late March/early April
Stout olive-brown body with dark slate-gray wings and short stubby tails. These flies tend to ride low in or on the surface film for some distance before taking flight. Emerger.

QUILL GORDON – LIMITED
#12; Early April
Light gray with darker rings on abdomen and pale-gray wings. Emerger.

HENDRICKSON/RED QUILL – WIDESPREAD
#12-14; April 1-15
Female: (Hendrickson) are the larger of the species; the body is a grayish tan with pink highlights and a medium-gray wing. Male: (red quill) have a rusty-brown body and medium-gray wing. Emerger and Adult.

BLUE QUILL – LIMITED
#16-18; April 1-15
Rusty-brown body with slate-gray wings. Emerger.

LIGHT HENDRICKSON – LIMITED
#14; Late April
Light tannish-yellow body and pale, smoky wings. Emerger and Adult.

MARCH BROWN/GRAY FOX – LIMITED
#10-14; May 1-25
Tan/brown body with amber wings mottled with darker spots. Emerger.

PALE EVENING DUN/SULPHUR – WIDESPREAD
#16-18; May 25-June 30
Light yellow to dark sulphur body with pale-gray wings. Emerger and Adult.

LIGHT CAHILL – COMMON

#14-16; May-June

Light creamy-tan body with pale wings. Adult.

SLATE DRAKE – WIDESPREAD

#10-14; May-September

Deep brownish with a hint of purple body and dark slate-gray wings. Nymph and Adult.

YELLOW DRAKE – LIMITED

#10; June-July

Yellow body with creamy yellow wings. Adult.

TRICO – COMMON

#20-24; Mid June through July

Male: Dark gray/black body, pale-gray wing. Female: Pale gray-green body, pale-gray wing. Adult and Spinner.

TINY BLUE-WINGED OLIVE – WIDESPREAD

#20-24; August to October

Dark brownish olive with slate-gray wings. Emerger and Adult.

Caddisflies

Caddisfly species out-number mayfly species by a wide margin, yet we know much more about the latter. All you have to do for proof is go to any bookstore or fly shop and check out the books, you will see a couple of books on caddisflies and many on mayflies. Maybe that is because there are so many species of caddisflies that it seems a daunting task to separate them and understand when, how and where each may hatch. Yet they are so prevalent I almost expect to see caddis on the water or in the air every time I step into a river or stream. They are that common.

To the uneducated eye, a caddis looks much like a small, tent-winged moth so common in the summer months flitting around porch lights and the fluorescent lights of 24-hour gas stations. The primary difference in the adult is that a moth's wings are covered with micro scales that will come off on your fingers like powder and they have short, feathery antennae, while a caddis has two sets of wings that are covered with tiny hairs (that don't come off) and long, thin hair-like antennae.

In flight, the caddis appears as a clumsy mass of moving wings with no apparent flight pattern or destination. One of the keys to size identification is to understand that in flight the insect appears one and sometimes two sizes larger than it actually is. I call this phenomenon the "illusion of movement"—the movement of the four wings creates an illusion that the insect is much larger than it is. I believe this is what many fishermen experience as selectivity in the trout's feeding behavior, when in fact it is nothing more than the angler seeing the insect in flight and choosing an imitation that is too large. It might be the same color, but it is larger than the natural. When this occurs you will hear the familiar sounds of frustrated anglers who know they have the right imitation but blame the fish as being too selective expecting a most life-like imitation, when in fact the solution is as easy as going down a size or two. Of course, you can always grab one of the insects out of the air and look at it up close and personal before tying on your imitation.

There are over 1350 species of caddis in North America but fortunately for the angler it is not necessary to know even a fraction of them in detail. The majority can be imitated with four or five main color combinations, with size being the only other critical factor when imitating them. In Gary LaFontaine's ground-breaking book, *Caddisflies*, he even goes so far as to offer four primary color variations to cover seventy percent of the situations an angler will encounter when fishing caddisflies. Even so, the specific caddisflies and their imitations that follow are the most common in the Northeast and Midwest, and therefore, in order to fish these hatches most successfully the fly-fisherman should have some working knowledge of them.

There are four stages in the life cycle of the caddisfly: larva, pupa, adult and egg laying. It is important that the angler understand each of these stages in order to identify which stage the trout may or may not be feeding on at any given time so they can choose the best imitation for that situation. Because the larvae live under the surface on the various rocks, stones, and other substrate, it is the only stage you do not imitate actively, but instead you fish imitations that resemble the species of caddis in the waters you are fishing. When trout are feeding on one of the other stages, the observant angler is usually able to identify which stage the trout are feeding on. Lastly, caddisflies only have one generation per year.

The Musconetcong River just down river from Hackettstown was where I had one of my most memorable days fishing a caddis hatch in New Jersey. It was a warm late-April afternoon under an unusually hazy sun for that time of year. The trees lining the river banks were still bare except for the round purple-green buds forming at the ends of their branches and the forsythia beneath them were in their full yellow glory. The river was clear and just right; the riffle I was standing in had small ripples on the surface that were just high enough to hide my tippet, the water was about knee deep. In the air and on the water was a blizzard of dusky-colored grannom caddis. They were everywhere, getting in my eyes and ears and on the water in good numbers.

As the caddisflies increased in number so did the number of trout that were rising. I had my pick of fish as I stood at the tail of the run looking upstream. The trout were porpoising and slashing the water surface as they took the emerging caddis. There was no doubt about where they were and what they were taking. Along the right bank there was a deeper slick about forty feet long and about six feet wide that had three or four nice fish working. Above me and to the top of the riffle in the middle section there were perhaps a dozen to eighteen smaller trout taking flies off the top. This is typical in a situation like this; the larger fish will take up the best feeding lies, and the smaller, less dominant trout were in the middle of the river exposed to predators and the whim of the wind.

To my left the river was shallow except just off the rocky shoreline where there was a very deep, narrow vein of water that had two fish lazily sipping injured caddis off the top. This was typical, too, for this was the best feeding lie and these were the biggest fish. The bushes above the rocks shaded the run nicely and made the water dark opaque, perfect to hide from predators.

My heart was pounding in my chest and it was difficult to concentrate as I tied a Dorado Hare's Ear dry fly to the end of my 5X tippet. Just about the same time the year before, I had met an elderly fly-fisherman in this same stretch of water who said this was the fly to use when the grannom caddis came off. He gave me one, this one, and said to keep it because he was sure that I would hit this hatch right some time. A year later, no truer words were spoken.

I was 17 at the time and still fairly green, and with all these fish rising around me it was hard to decide where to cast. I saw the big trout rising over on the left bank and I saw the nice fish rising along the right bank. The smaller trout working the riffle above me were vying for my attention as they noisily chased down the hatching caddis. And of course, there were the fish along the right bank. Then one of the big trout on the left bank came up and took a caddis in a loud GULP! My mind was made up for me.

I turned to my right and began false casting, lengthening the amount of line outside my rod tip with each forward cast. When I thought I had enough line and leader out to reach a spot about two feet above where the trout last rose, I made one more back cast before pushing the rod, and then the line behind it, toward my target. The fly landed a little short but I lowered my rod tip to make the most of the cast. The current caught the line between me and the fly and began to drag the fly towards me just as it drifted to the side of where the trout was. I thought I had screwed up when I saw this, but just as I was ready to lift my line off the water, this big maw came out of the darkness and engulfed the fly.

The second that monster felt the hook in its jaw, it bolted downstream just under the surface making a V wake behind it. It kept going, too, over the rock weir separating this pool from the one below. I just held on with my rod in a deep arc and the reel singing as the click drag purred on. And he kept going, and going until I ran out of line and backing and when the line tightened because there was no more on the reel, the fly popped out of its jaw and my line sprung back at me like a rubber band that just broke. What a rush!

Yes, the big one got away that day. But after I managed to calm down, I did catch a number of the other trout working in that pool. All of them brown trout and every one of them took the Dorado Hare's Ear fly given to me a year before just for this occasion.

Caddis Larvae – Caddis larvae are small grub-like worms with six legs located immediately behind a tiny dark head. There are two kinds of caddis larvae living in our streams—cased caddis larvae and free-living caddis larvae. One interesting thing about some caddis is that they will spin webs in front of themselves to trap food moving in the current.

The various cased caddis larvae that inhabit New Jersey rivers and streams should be imitated. These caddis larvae live in cases made out of either small stones or grains of sand, little twigs, or pieces of leaves and other wood parts such as bark; others have spun silk-like cases. Each genus of caddis is easily identified by its case, as even those that make their cases out of the same material will make it in a different shape than another genus. You don't really need to know which caddis builds which case; you just need to have a general imitation of cased caddis larvae. One of the simplest patterns is the Strawman

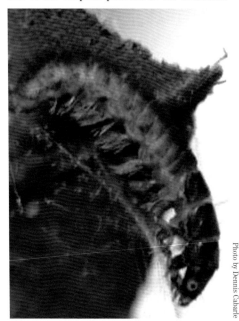

Caddis larva.

Photo by Dennis Cabarle

nymph. I will show you several, including this one, in the fly patterns chapter.

There is really only one type of free-living caddis larvae in New Jersey waters and it is commonly called the green rockworm. The rockworm is in the genus *Rhyacophila*. As its familiar name suggests, it is a green, sometimes bright green, larvae that lives in the fast riffles and pocket water of our streams and is found clinging to the downstream side of boulders and stones. Because they do not live in a case (free-living) like most other caddis larvae, and therefore are exposed as they crawl along the rocks of the stream bottom, they are especially vulnerable to the trout. The trout know them well and look for them because they regularly lose their grip and tumble free in the water column throughout the season. This is an important insect to imitate.

The surest way to tell if caddisflies are hatching is that you will see trout rising and no insects on the water. You may see plenty of flies in the air flitting about, but none on water, yet trout are bulging, porpoising, or coming clear out of the water as they chase the ascending pupae.

Caddis Pupae – Shortly before the caddis larvae are ready hatch into adults, they will pupate by tucking their heads into their case and closing off the opening. The free-living caddis larvae will build a silken case around itself to pupate. To understand this better think of the butterfly, the caterpillar builds a cocoon around itself and develops from its wormlike self into a winged butterfly. The caddis larva does the same thing except under water. The most important part of the pupal stage for the angler is when the pupa has fully formed into an adult and swims to the surface to fly off. They are extremely vulnerable at this point as they are fully exposed as they ascend the water column. Once at the surface some caddis will penetrate the meniscus and immediately fly off, while others will struggle to free themselves of the pupal shuck just under the surface, becoming an even easier target for the hungry trout.

Therefore, the emergent pupae are an extremely important stage of the caddisfly life cycle for the fly-fisherman to imitate. There are the traditional wet flies, which are seldom used by the modern angler, although the soft-hackle wet fly certainly does have its place in most anglers fly boxes. I will recommend several later in the fly patterns chapter.

There are many different emergent caddis patterns that closely imitate the natural insect. Some of these imitations have wing pads and legs on them and while they do work, I prefer using the LaFontaine Emergent Sparkle Pupa and Emerger. It is very effective and covers a wide range of situations. There are only four colors the angler will need to imitate the majority of caddis in our rivers and streams.

There is one fly pattern you will need to imitate the unique pupal behavior of a specific caddisfly species. When hatching, the pupae of the cinnamon caddis drift helplessly in the surface film for brief periods as they free themselves from the pupal skin. This trait created a need for a specific pattern to mimic this behavior, which led to the creation of the Iris Caddis by Craig Mathews and John Juracek. The Iris Caddis is a fairly simple pattern that uses a horizontal loop of Z-lon over the abdomen to imitate the emerging down wing of the caddisfly. It is a deadly pattern I wouldn't fish any trout stream without.

This imitation of the pupal stage of the cinnamon caddis is important because it hatches from our rivers and streams from May through September. Most species of this caddis hatch in the evening, although some do hatch in the afternoon. The key to knowing when to fish the Iris Caddis is when you see the caddis, light tan-brown in color, flying erratically as they always do a few feet over the water but you won't see any on the water. This is because the pupa literally goes from the water surface into the air. They don't sit even for a second on the water after hatching. Fish the imitation just as you would a dry fly—dead-drift it right in the surface film.

Adult Caddis – Adult caddisflies emerge so quickly from the pupa that they are rarely available to trout during a hatch. Most adults live for several weeks after hatching living in the streamside trees and shrubs. During this time they fall or get blown onto the water and quite often become a meal for an alert trout. This happens often enough that the trout are aware of their presence and they will be looking for them. For this reason, the trout angler should carry adult caddis imitations. Again, you will only need them in a few colors and various sizes to cover most situations when on stream.

Egg-Laying Caddis – When female caddisflies return to the river to lay their eggs it brings even the wariest trout to the surface to feed. Like everything else about caddisflies, there is no rule of thumb for fishing to rising trout when they are feeding on egg-layers. The reason for this is because female caddis lay there in a different manner depending on the species. There are four primary methods of egg laying: 1) Some will fall on the water surface and collapse spent on it, dropping their eggs when they do. 2) Others bounce on the water surface forcing the egg sac on the end of their abdomen through the meniscus where they release the eggs to drift to the bottom. Some anglers refer to these caddis as "popcorn caddis" 3) Others will fly to objects submerged in the water such as sticks, rocks, and even the legs of a wading fisherman, crawl down them on the downstream side and lay their eggs on them a short distance below the surface. You may have experienced this as it has happened to me many times while fishing in New Jersey in late May—you step out of the stream after fishing the evening rise and on your waders you will see a light green slime just under the top of the water line. 4) In many species of caddis the females will dive and swim down to the bottom to lay their eggs. When they get to the bottom they crawl around on the rocks and stones looking for the right place to lay their eggs. Some of them will even swim back to the surface and fly away.

The spent egg-layer is by far the easiest of the egg-layers to imitate. You fish it much like you would any dead-drifted dry fly. I like to use Lawson's Spent Caddis for these situations.

Fishing your fly to the bouncing egg-layers is a little tricky. Using a high-floating pattern and using your rod tip you cast your fly over rising trout and twitch the fly, or skitter it on the surface like the natural. Once you find the technique and speed the fish want, try to remember what you did as that will apply to the entire evening of fishing. For this type of fishing I have an egg-laying caddis pattern complete with an egg sac on the end of the abdomen.

Fishing to the diving and swimming egg-layers is a little more challenging. First you need to identify the behavior, which isn't always easy. Once you recognize that the trout are feeding on subsurface egg-laying caddis, fly selection becomes a matter of matching the size and color of the natural with a diving caddis imitation. I use the LaFontaine Diving Caddis; it's a very simple pattern that is very effective.

The following caddis hatches are the more common species found in New Jersey waters. I should also mention however, that there are many others that may be common in some waters and not in others. Lastly, when you see a pattern called a Little Olive Sedge, it is a caddisfly pattern. Sedge is another term for caddis used more commonly in the British Isles.

If you want to keep it simple, you can carry the four main color schemes Gary LaFontaine recommends in different sizes to match just about any caddis hatch you encounter in New Jersey. I have listed the color patterns for each stage—pupa, emerger, adult, and egg-layer—in the fly patterns chapter. The choice is yours.

Caddisfly Hatches – The following are the common names of the more important caddisflies that hatch in New Jersey along with their size, hatch calendar, and descriptions for identifying the adult.

GRANNOM
#14-16; Early April through May
Species #1: Dark-gray body with lighter lateral stripe and dark-gray wings.
Species #2: Apple green body with mottled brown wings.

DUN OLIVE CADDIS
#14-16; Late April through May
Olive-green body with gray wings

LITTLE OLIVE SEDGE
#18-22; May through September
Olive-green body with gray-brown wings.

CINNAMON CADDIS
#14-18; May through September
Cinnamon brown body with grayish wings with tan spots.

DARK BLUE SEDGE
#14-16; Late April through June
Greenish-black body with dark blue-gray wings.

BROWN LONGHORN SEDGE
#16-18; Summer evenings
Reddish-brown body with darker wings.

GREEN SEDGE (ROCKWORM)
#14-16; Sporadic May through September
Green body with gray wings mottled with tan spots.

BOX-WING SEDGE
#14-18; May through September
Brownish-gray body and wings.

GREAT BROWN AUTUMN SEDGE
#8-10; September
Reddish-amber body with amber wings.

Stoneflies

Prehistoric looking is probably the best way to describe the stonefly, especially the nymph, or larval stage. A stonefly nymph looks like it is covered with armor plating from head to tail. The scientific name for the stonefly is Plecoptera, which means folded wings, because the adult stonefly's four wings (two on each side) fold together at rest and lay flat along their back looking as though it has only one big wing. As their common name suggests, the stonefly lives primarily in streams that are full of stones and rocks. They require fast-flowing, clean, clear water that is highly oxygenated. In fact, stoneflies are a good indicator of water quality—the more stoneflies that inhabit a stream, the better the water quality, and vice versa. They are found mostly in small rocky mountain streams and larger rivers surrounded by forest in the faster riffles and runs, but they can also be found in slower, highly oxygenated streams such as many spring creeks are.

Photo by Dennis Cabarle

Golden stonefly nymph.

So let's start with those fascinating looking nymphs. Depending on the species, stoneflies live in the nymphal stage anywhere from three months to three years before hatching into winged adults. They range in size from 1/4 to 2 1/2 inches long and are characterized by their two hair-like tails, two sets of wing pads on their thorax, six legs and two antennae. Their gills are under the thorax and around the base of their legs. Their body is relatively flat, slender and long compared to their width, which allows them to cling tightly to the bottom of rocks and stones where they feed on leaves and aquatic vegetation. Some are predatory however.

Most of the time stonefly nymphs are dark in coloration during this stage. They are found in three colors, or I should say some shade of one of three colors. There are black, brown and golden colored stoneflies depending on species. The golden stonefly nymphs in particular will have dark mottling on the back of their abdomen and wing pads, some strikingly beautiful. During the period they are in the nymphal stage they will molt every so often just as a snake outgrows its skin when it gets too big for it. When this happens the newly-skinned nymphs are a creamy white color for a short period of time. I like to fish a white stonefly nymph just for this reason where they are abundant, particularly during the warmer months when they are growing rapidly.

When the nymphs are mature and ready to hatch they will migrate along the stream bottom from the deeper runs and riffles to streamside rocks and boulders before crawling out on them and shedding their nymphal skin. You may have seen their empty shucks dried out and still clinging to rocks near fast riffles or pocket water just above the high-water mark. The newly hatched adults then fly into the streamside vegetation where they are unavailable to the trout until they return to the stream to lay their eggs.

The tiny black stoneflies and the early brown and black stoneflies are the exception to this rule as some manage to hatch like the mayflies. They hatch from mid-winter to early spring during the midday hours, sometimes on very cold, bright days. Their dark coloration serves its purpose very well as it absorbs the energy of the sun allowing them to hatch in sub-freezing temperatures. Some will crawl out of the water and hatch on the streamside rocks, while others will migrate to the calmer, shallow areas of the stream edge and swim to the surface where they break free of the nymphal shuck and fly away. Well, sort of, it's more like they are drunk, they are such clumsy fliers. If there is a breeze they get blown down to the water surface and skitter and tumble along. If there's a hungry trout in the vicinity many times it will launch itself up from the bottom to grab the hapless insect, its momentum carrying it clear of the water.

At the same time there are tiny black stoneflies and the early brown and black stoneflies hatching you may also see others returning to the water to lay their eggs. This is one of my favorite times of year to fish dry flies. When the winter stoneflies return to lay their eggs they will fly down to the water and skim along it dropping their eggs, creating a soft V wake on the surface. If the water is clear and the sun is out the trout will come out of their winter doldrums to chase these clumsy fliers and grab them with ferocity, throwing water and making a minor racket. The stoneflies seem to prefer certain areas of a stream for this activity, making it easier for the angler to concentrate on one spot. When this happens I put on an adult stonefly imitation and stand upstream and across from the action and drop my fly above where the trout are attacking the egg-layers. The first few times my fly drifts into the zone I will dead-drift it

Little black stonefly adult.

Photo by Dennis Cabarle

over the fish. If that does not work, I will lift my rod tip once the fly gets to the lower end of the zone, skittering the fly over the water surface like the naturals. Many times the trout will hammer the fly, grabbing it and hooking themselves.

The four or five other species of stoneflies that inhabit New Jersey waters are rarely available to the trout as adults. In all my years of trout fishing in the state I have only seen egg-laying by the later season stoneflies twice and only once were there enough to bring trout to the surface to take them. But because these stoneflies are large and live in the stream for sometimes more than a year, the trout are accustomed to seeing them get washed out of their lairs into the water column. They tumble and twist in the current and because they are a big meal, they get the attention of the trout. I highly recommend you carry and fish the large stonefly nymph imitations in the faster stretches and pocket water of our rivers and streams.

There are only a few species of stoneflies that are present in any numbers in New Jersey rivers and streams. Except for the tiny black and the early brown and black stoneflies, you will rarely see adults on the water and available to the trout. However, I strongly recommend you carry and fish the nymphs because they are a big, protein-packed meal for the trout.

Stonefly Hatches

TINY BLACK STONEFLY
#14-18; Mid February through March
Black body with soft-gray wings – very slender.

EARLY BLACK STONEFLY
#10-12; Late February into March
Grayish-black body with smoky wings.

EARLY BROWN STONEFLY
#10-12; March into early April
Brown to reddish-brown body with smoky wings.

GIANT BROWN STONEFLY
#6-8; Late May through June
Medium chocolate brown body with heavily-veined wings.

GOLDEN STONEFLY
#6; June-July Nocturnal
Golden-yellow body with very light amber wings.

LITTLE YELLOW STONEFLY
#10-12; June through July
Yellow body with pale-yellow wings.

Midges

These tiny two-winged aquatic insects are a very important part of every trout's diet. They are found in just about every type of trout water as they have a wide range of tolerance when it comes to water quality. Trout feed on the larva, pupa and the adult stage, although in New Jersey we generally concentrate on the adult or emergent stage when trout fishing. One other reason they are important to the angler is that they are available throughout the year, hatching in all kinds of weather. Of course, there is a trade-off; midges are typically very small and hard to see for many anglers, including myself. There was a time though, before I needed glasses, that I fished midges all the time and did quite well with them. Now I only use them when I know that's what the trout are feeding on and the light is good.

Midge larvae look very much like brightly colored, small, clearly segmented worms and depending on the species, they may be black, red, olive, cream, gray, green or tan. When I say small, I mean a large midge may be a size 18 standard-shank hook, but they average more like #20-24 hook. Some are even smaller, if you can believe that. They live on the stream bottom in plant beds, mud, sand and other soft or decaying bottom materials.

When the midge larvae are ready to pupate they develop a pupal case around themselves and undergo their transformation from a worm-like larva to a winged, six-legged insect. Then they rise or swim from the bottom and hang just under the surface and drift as they split their pupal shuck, wiggle out, and then sit on the surface drying their wings before flying away. It is at this point, when they are hanging just under the surface, that they are most susceptible to the trout. Think: they are just like the caddis but much smaller.

The adult midge is a curious insect in that it tends to cluster together when hatching, creating these little masses of several insects that ride the water surface. The trout will feed on these clumps as opposed to individual insects because they get more bang for their buck. I have seen trout cruising just under the surface in calm water lifting their head every time they come to a midge cluster to sip it in. Sometimes they will take a half dozen or more clumps before descending to the bottom, falling back a short ways, and then rising up to do it all over again.

Terrestrials

Ants – I do not think I have ever seen a trout that did not like a nice tasty ant for a summertime snack. And there is a good reason for that – there are more ants on this planet than any other insect or animal group. They are literally everywhere, making them a regular part of a trout's diet no matter what river or stream they live in. But ants are terrestrial insects, which is why they do not make up the bulk of a trout's diet, despite their abundance. The various ants a trout sees in its lifetime may be small black ones, big black ones, small red or cinnamon ones, and some that are red and black. For this reason ants are a good searching pattern on days when nothing is hatching and you just have to fish dry flies. The one interesting thing about ant patterns is that there are so many of them, despite the fact that all ants look exactly the same except for size and color. I have seen ants with bodies made from fur, balsa, foam, thread, dubbed CDC, and deer hair. Some ants are tied with wings, and others have fluorescent orange poly or another bright material on their back for visibility. Lastly, not all ant patterns are tied to float; a sunken or drowned ant pattern can be very effective at times also.

There are certain times of the year when ants do become available to trout in large numbers, much like a hatch of mayflies or caddisflies. This occurs when ants leave their nests to go on their annual mating flights to create new colonies. When this happens near a trout stream tens of thousands of winged ants fill the air over the river where many of them fall to the water because they are spent or blown in by wind. Trout key in on the ants and sometimes it looks like every trout in the river is rising. Obviously, a winged ant pattern of the appropriate size is killer in these circumstances.

There are times when an ant is the appropriate fly to tie on the end of your tippet; generally on warm, breezy days when you see no insects flying about in the air, or riding the water surface, but you see trout rising. The rises will be very soft and come just after a gust of wind under trees and other vegetation hanging over the water. What is happening is the breeze is blowing ants (sometimes beetles) out of the branches and onto the water. Sometimes you can scan the water surface and you will see the ants, making it easy to choose the right color and size. Other times you will have to use the old trial-and-error method. I like to start with a small black ant when I'm guessing, especially if I can't see anything on the water, because that usually means whatever it is the trout are taking is very small. I also have a foam-bodied pattern I call the Antbeetle, just for these occasions.

One of the other things about ants and terrestrials in general is that they are good hatch busters. Let's say you are fishing a late afternoon or early evening Sulphur hatch and despite your best efforts and having the "right" fly on to match the hatch, you are getting refusal after refusal. When you start to think you're going crazy, stop and think terrestrial or ant, and tie one on. Many times you will be pleasantly surprised at the results. The trout take the ant like candy, even those that are clearly taking the small yellow duns.

Beetles – There may not be as many beetles as there are ants on the planet, but there are many, many more kinds of beetles than there are ants. Even still, they do occur in great enough numbers that they can be found just about anywhere when the ambient temperatures remain above freezing. One can safely assume that the streamside vegetation is crawling with beetles of varying sizes, shapes and colors. And like the ant, they are continually getting blown out of the shrubbery and onto the water. Unlike the ant, beetles are a meaty morsel that will pull trout to them like a magnet, sometimes from pretty far away.

Beetles mostly hang out in the lower shrubs along the stream banks, so that is where you should concentrate your efforts when fishing a beetle pattern. I like to fish a beetle when nothing is hatching and the rivers are not too high or off color.

Sometimes you can find trout holding along the bank and sight-fish to them, and even if they are not feeding, a properly placed beetle will bring them up to take it. Either way, I will wade out to the center of a long pool or run and work my way up stream fishing a beetle in the water from right off the bank to about ten feet out. I alternate my casts from one bank to the other and cover lots of water as I move up to the head of the run.

Grasshoppers – In some years grasshoppers, or hoppers as they are more commonly called, are more abundant than in others. But they are rarely as important to the New Jersey angler as they are to anglers fishing Midwestern or Western trout streams. It will also depend on the terrain a river is flowing through as to whether hoppers will be an important food source. Rivers flowing through wooded valleys and mountainous areas will have few if any grasshoppers living along their banks. While rivers flowing through farmland valleys and open fields will have an abundance of hoppers, and therefore, the trout will be accustomed to feeding on them.

Grasshoppers are seasonal insects that start to show in late July, peak in mid-August, and stick around until the first frost, usually some time in September. They are one of the largest insects that most trout will see in their lifetime, some are as large as an inch and a half in length. They are also bulky, offering the trout a serious meal even having just one.

And how do they wind up in the water? Some just hop or fly over the stream and fall short of their destination, assuming it is the other side. On windy days they get blown onto the water. Either way, because they are so big, when they land on the water it makes quite a splash that instantly draws the attention of nearby trout. And because they are a big struggling insect making lots of commotion on the surface, the trout usually waste no time attacking them. The way a trout slams a hopper is the source of many great fishing stories. I have had good hopper fishing on the Musconetcong River, the Pequest, and on certain sections of the South Branch of the Raritan River.

Crickets – Crickets are active through the warmer months of the season and there are enough of them that land on the water to warrant carrying imitations in your fly box. Like the grasshopper, they are found primarily in stretches of river that meander through farmland and open fields, although I have caught trout using them on streams flowing through forested land.

Inch Worms – In late spring, when those bright-green inch worms begin to suspend themselves from the tree branches on their fine silken lines, the trout are on the alert for them. They average about 1/2 to 3/4 of an inch long and are hairless. For the few short weeks these caterpillars are active, fishing an appropriate imitation will usually bring positive results. I recommend that you carry both floating and sinking patterns.

Other Aquatic Foods

Scuds/Freshwater Shrimp – Scuds are one of the most important food sources for trout in New Jersey rivers and streams. They thrive in just about every trout stream in the state where trout are found. Scuds look very much like a small shrimp with their curved, segmented bodies, fourteen pairs of legs and antennae dangling under their body. They also can move backwards and forwards and even swim upside down at times. Scuds vary in color, but most often are some shade of gray olive to tannish olive to a pink tan. They range in size from a size 12 down to a size 18.

They prefer aquatic weed beds in slower stretches of river, either along the banks or at the bottom of deep, slow runs and pools. They can also be found in the gravel of the stream bed feeding on green plant matter. Trout are very fond of scuds and will feed on them every chance they get. And because they are very active swimmers and crawlers, they are easy targets for opportunistic fish. Trout also seem to know that scuds are a good source of protein and they will seek them out when they need a pick-me-up. This is one fly I would not be without when fishing a New Jersey trout stream.

Forage Fish – Trout, especially big trout, love to feed on minnows, dace, darters and sculpins, as they offer lots of protein in one bite. Big fish need a big meal to sustain their size and maintain an energy level needed for their continued growth. Mayflies, caddisflies and other insects are good for a snack or a light meal when they are present in high numbers, but a single minnow can fill their belly in one bite. So if you want to significantly increase the number of large trout you catch, fish streamers and other minnow imitations more often.

Forage fish are found in just about every river and stream that trout inhabit. There are all kinds of minnows and small forage fish present in New Jersey waters, some are bright, silvery fish, and others tend to be mottled similarly to the river bottom color. They range in size, at least the sizes the trout prefer, from one inch to four inches. When startled, some swim in short, quick bursts, while others dart around frantically and still others motor up or down stream to the next run or pool.

Knowing that forage fish are varied in size, color and behavior is the key to fishing the imitations properly. You should carry some patterns that are bright with prominent eyes and others that are mottled and subdued in color. Because we usually fish streamers and other minnow imitations actively, weighted patterns are best to make sure your fly gets down deep where the big fish are found.

Crayfish – The crayfish is an important item in every large trout's diet. Looking like small lobsters, they live among the rocks, gravel and vegetation on the river bed where they can burrow or find shelter in tight places in the rocks. Crayfish are nocturnal creatures, which works well for large trout, as they are night predators as well. Like the scud, they can move forwards and backwards. Under normal circumstances, crayfish crawl both forwards and backwards. But when in danger they use their wide curving tail to swim in reverse in rapid bursts of speed to the nearest shelter. The imitation should be fished by stripping it back to you, varying the length and speed of the strip with each cast to mimic this behavior.

Royal Wulff dry fly.

Notes on Fly Tying

I have been fly-tying several years longer than I have been fly-fishing for trout. The first few years I tested my flies on bluegills, sunnies, small bass, and other pan fish on a tiny brook in New Vernon. Many of my first flies were wet flies and streamers from the classic Ray Bergman book, *Trout*. My tying vise, tools and materials were very basic and came in a single small box along with a spool of black thread (no bobbin), and a cake of beeswax. After each material was tied in with a few wraps, you had to tie a couple half hitches over them to keep the thread from unraveling. I had a fly-pattern book full of bright plates with flies that were more artistic and colorful than they were imitative, with names like Royal Coachman, McGinty, Professor and Mickey Finn. I was self-taught and so I developed a style over time that was practical and precise. I read everything I could get my hands on and practiced every day for years. So you will note that my technique is both similar to most other tiers yet different at the same time.

Over the years I have found that a sparsely tied fly is usually more effective than a heavily dressed one. I use 6/0 olive Danville pre-waxed thread for 90% of my tying because I feel that it blends in best with most materials and the hook. It looks right to me. I rarely incorporate weight into my flies using wire under the body because every nymph I have ever seen drifting in the current appears to be weightless. But I do use bead heads on some of my nymphs and they fish quite well. I know you may be shaking your head right now thinking that does not make sense, but without the bead a weighted nymph does not jive with what I have seen with my eyes. Of course, I have never seen a live nymph with a bright, golden helmet on its head either. It's all about confidence that comes from tying your flies the way you believe they will look best to the trout and therefore work the best.

If you tie your own flies, use your head as well as your hands. By this I mean that as you are tying a fly, think in your mind's eye about how it will look **IN** or **ON** the water and how you will fish it once you tie it on the end of your tippet. This way you will create a fly that works with your style of fishing both physically and mentally so when you get to the stream you will have already fished all of your flies in your mind. You will already know it will fish as you want it to, and that confidence in the fly you are fishing is the single most important aspect of being a successful fly-fisherman.

So what else is important when tying flies? First of all, you must maintain the proper proportions of the various materials you are tying with as they relate to the size of the hook. Color is important as is the silhouette of the finished fly as it relates to the natural you are imitating. If the fly you are tying is a general imitation or attractor, keep your proportions accurate, i.e., if it is a nymph, the abdomen should be 2/3 of body length, and the thorax 1/3. If the nymph you are tying has legs (hackle) keep it sparse—insects only have six or eight legs at the most. Same with the tails, most nymphs have two or three tails at most, so do not tie in a dozen fibers on a pheasant tail nymph or hare's ear.

When tying dry flies that have hackle in them, do not over hackle—making too many turns—the fly. It may look cool and stand up better on your tying table, but too many hackle wraps can create too much drag when casting the fly. This drag makes the fly twist, which then may twist your tippet, especially if it is too light. This is something you will learn by trial and error as every tier has a different vision of how their fly should look, and because hackle barb count and quality varies with each neck. It is safe to say that with good-quality hackle, you should have no more than 3, maybe 4 turns of hackle on large flies, at most on each side of the wing on a traditional Catskill style dry fly. With a thorax style dry no more than 2, maybe 3 turns of hackle on larger flies, at most on each side of the wing.

You should also use the best tools and materials that you can afford. Your vise should be solid and hold a hook securely. Scissors have to be sharp with good points. Hackle pliers must hold a hackle tight so it doesn't slip out just as you are finishing wrapping it and have to start all over again, but not so tight that it breaks it. And lastly, flatten the barbs down on your hooks before you tie the fly on them. If you wait until the fly is tied or until you get to the stream and you break it, you will have wasted your time.

The following fly patterns are those that I have had the most success with over the years for Garden State trout. While certainly not the only patterns you can use in New Jersey, they have served me well. For additional effective patterns check with your favorite fly shop, fishing buddy, web site, or make up your own.

Scud/Freshwater Shrimp

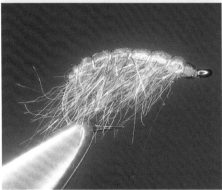

Hook: Scud #12-16
Thread: Olive
Rib: Fine gold wire
Shellback: Clear scudback or pearlescent mylar for flashback scud
Dubbing: Mixed medium red fox squirrel fur, olive rabbit and clear Antron fibers: 2:1:1 ratio

Beadhead Pheasant Tail Nymph

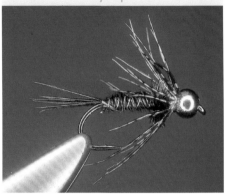

Hook: Nymph #10-16 mounted with a gold bead
Thread: Black
Tail: Pheasant-tail fibers
Rib: Fine copper wire
Body: Pheasant-tail fibers
Thorax: Peacock herl
Hackle: Hungarian partridge wound as a collar behind gold bead

New Jersey Fly Patterns

Pheasant Tail Nymph

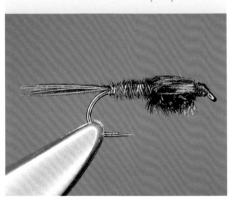

Hook: Nymph #10-24
Thread: Brown
Tail: Pheasant-tail fibers
Rib: Copper wire
Wing Case: Dark pheasant-tail fibers
Thorax: Pheasant-tail fibers or peacock herl
Legs: Pheasant-tail fibers (optional)

Gold Ribbed Hare's Ear Nymph

Hook: Nymph #10-18
Thread: Olive
Tail: Woodduck flank fibers
Rib: Gold tinsel
Body: Hare's mask
Wing Case: Dark mottled turkey tail
Thorax: Hare's mask picked out

Vinnie's Isonychia Nymph

Hook: Nymph #10-12
Thread: Black
Tail: 3 peacock sword herls clipped short; about 1 hook gap in length
Body: Mixed claret, brown and black dubbing in a 2:1:1 ratio
Rib: Fine copper wire
Wing Case: Dark turkey tail
Thorax: Same as body
Legs: Dark speckled partridge

Prince Nymph

Hook: Nymph #10-16
Thread: Black
Tail: Dark brown goose biots
Body: Peacock herl
Rib: Oval gold
Wing: 2 white goose biots
Hackle: Dark brown

Zug Bug

Hook: Nymph #12-16
Thread: Black
Tail: Peacock sword tips, 3
Rib: Oval silver
Body: Peacock herl
Hackle: Brown
Wing Case: Mallard flank tied in at head over body and clipped 1/3 of the way back

Caddis Larva (Rockworm)

Hook: Scud #14-16
Thread: Black
Tail: None
Rib: Fine gold wire (optional)
Abdomen: Caddis green synthetic dubbing
Thorax: Black dubbing
Note: I also tie these with a rusty yellow body/dark brown thorax, tan body/dark brown thorax, and medium brown body/dark brown head to represent other common species.

White Larva

Hook: Scud #16-22
Thread: Black
Body: White ice dubbing
Head: Black dubbing
Note: This simple nymph works well as a dropper behind a larger nymph. It imitates a wide variety of aquatic larvae.

LaFontaine Sparkle Caddis Pupa

Hook: Dry fly #12-18
Thread: 6/0 Black
Trailing Shuck: Medium olive sparkle yarn
Under Body: Bright green dubbed sparkle yarn
Over Body: Medium olive sparkle yarn
Legs: Hungarian partridge fibers
Thorax: Brown dubbing
Note: This fly should also be tied in three other main colors: Brown/yellow, and dark gray and ginger.

Stonefly Nymph

Hook: Streamer or nymph, size to match natural
Thread: To match body
Tails: Goose biots to match body
Abdomen: Fur dubbed to match body
Rib: V-rib to match body
Wing Cases: Light or dark mottled turkey tail to match body
Thorax: Fur dubbed to match body
Antennae: Goose biots to match body
Recommended colors: Black, brown or golden yellow

Emergers

Blue Winged Olive

Hook: Dry fly #14-22
Thread: Olive
Tail: Medium dun hackle fibers, short
Emerging Wing: Gray polypropylene ball
Body: Dark brownish olive

Sulphur - Emerger

Hook: Dry fly #16-20
Thread: Yellow
Tail: Amber Z-lon fibers
Wing: Tuft of snowshoe rabbit foot fibers
Body: Creamy yellow to olive yellow

Quill Gordon

Hook: Dry fly #12-14
Thread: Olive
Tail: Woodduck flank fibers
Body: Medium hare's ear dubbing picked out in front third
Rib: Gold tinsel
Wing: Gray goose quills or snowshoe rabbit foot fibers tied back over body.

Iris Caddis

Hook: TMC 102Y #15-17
Thread: 6/0 Tan
Trailing Shuck: Amber Z-lon
Body: Mixed tan fur and clear Antron 2:1
Emerging Wing: White Z-lon looped horizontally over abdomen
Thorax: Medium hare's ear touch-dubbed

LaFontaine Sparkle Caddis Emerger

Hook: Dry fly #12-18
Thread: 6/0 Black
Trailing Shuck: Gold sparkle yarn (Antron)
Under Body: Mixed gold and brown dubbed Antron
Over Body: Gold sparkle yarn (Antron)
Wing: Brown mottled deer body hair
Thorax: Brown dubbing
Note: This fly should also be tied in the three other main colors: Brown/bright green, ginger, and dark gray.

Little Black Stonefly a.k.a. Dr. Seuss

Hook: Dry Fly #10-14
Thread: Black
Body: Black deer body hair
Wing: Goose primary quill tied to curve away from each other
Hackle: Dark dun

Dorado Hare's Ear

Hook: Dry Fly #12-16
Thread: Olive
Wing: Woodduck flank fibers; upright and divided
Tail: Guard hairs from hare's mask
Body: Rough hare's ear touch-dubbed
Hackle: One brown and one grizzly

Blue Winged Olive – Thorax

Hook: Dry fly #14-22
Thread: Olive
Tail: Medium dun hackle fibers or Micro Fibetts (split)
Wing: Upright natural gray CDC feather tips
Body: Dark brownish olive
Hackle: Medium to dark dun

Sulphur/Pale Evening Dun – Thorax

Hook: Dry fly #16-20
Thread: Yellow
Tail: Light or sandy dun hackle fibers
Wing: Upright natural gray CDC feather tips or dyed pale-gray turkey flats
Body: Creamy yellow to olive yellow
Hackle: Light or sandy dun

Hendrickson Usual

Hook: Dry fly #12-14
Thread: 6/0 Olive
Tail: Snowshoe rabbit foot guard hairs
Body: Mixed tan, gray and pink rabbit
Wing: Snowshoe rabbit foot hair
Note: I use this pattern more than any other mayfly dun imitation; just use the appropriate hook size, thread, and body color for the mayfly you want to represent and use snowshoe rabbit for the tail and wing. It is a very simple, yet very effective pattern that may be taken as an emerger, cripple or dun.

Light Cahill

Hook: Dry fly #1-16
Thread: Tan or cream
Wing: Woodduck flank fibers; upright and divided
Tail: Tan or cream hackle fibers
Body: Light tan or cream hackle fibers
Hackle: Cream or light ginger

Grobert's Light Caddis Adult

Hook: Dry fly #16-18
Thread: Tan
Body: Cream rabbit and clear Antron; 2:1 ratio
Under Wing: White or clear Z-lon
Wing: Light deer body hair or caribou hair
Thorax: Light or bleached English hare's ear touch-dubbed

Grobert's Medium Caddis Adult

Hook: Dry fly #12-18
Thread: Olive or brown
Body: Mix of medium brown and olive rabbit and clear Antron fibers: 1:1:1
Under Wing: White or clear Z-lon
Wing: Medium deer body hair or caribou hair
Thorax: Medium English hare's ear touch-dubbed

Grobert's Dark Caddis Adult

Hook: Dry fly #16-18
Thread: Olive
Body: Gray with a hint of olive and clear Antron; 2:1 ratio
Under Wing: White or clear Z-lon
Wing: Dark mottled deer body hair or caribou hair
Thorax: Medium English hare's ear touch-dubbed

Matt's Antbeetle

Hook: Dry fly #10-18
Thread: Black
Body: Black closed-cell foam
Legs: Moose body hair
Wing: Small tuft of dun or white CDC

Matt's Gnat – Midge Adult

Hook: Dry fly #16-24
Thread: Claret
Body: Peacock herl and snowshoe rabbit foot fibers twisted into a chenille-like rope and wrapped over the shank to front

Hook: Dry fly #12-14
Thread: Olive
Wing: Woodduck flank fibers or substitute, upright and divided
Tail: Medium dun hackle fibers
Body: Mixed gray, tan, and pink - 2:1:1
Hackle: Medium dun

Hook: Dry fly #12-14
Thread: Olive
Wing: Woodduck flank fibers or substitute, upright and divided
Tail: Medium dun hackle fibers
Body: Stripped brown hackle stem
Hackle: Medium dun

Hook: Dry fly #12-14
Thread: Olive
Wing: Woodduck flank fibers or substitute, upright and divided
Tail: Medium dun hackle fibers
Body: Stripped peacock quill or mixed gray and olive dubbing
Hackle: Medium dun

Hook: Dry fly #16-18
Thread: Olive
Wing: Upright gray CDC feather tips
Tail: Medium dun hackle fibers – split
Body: Reddish-brown dubbing
Hackle: Medium dun

New Jersey Fly Patterns

67

Light Hendrickson
a.k.a. Large Sulphur

Hook: Dry fly #12-14
Thread: Olive
Wing: Woodduck flank fibers or substitute, upright and divided
Tail: Light dun hackle fibers
Body: Light creamy yellow
Hackle: Light dun

March Brown/Gray Fox

Hook: Dry fly #10-14
Thread: Olive
Wing: Woodduck flank fibers or substitute, upright and divided
Tail: Mixed grizzly and brown
Body: Tannish brown
Hackle: One grizzly and one brown

Slate Drake – Thorax

Hook: Dry fly #10-12
Thread: Olive
Wing: Upright gray CDC feather tips
Tail: Medium dun hackle fibers – split
Body: Reddish-gray dubbing
Hackle: Medium dun

Yellow Drake – Thorax

Hook: Dry fly #10
Thread: Yellow
Wing: Upright creamy yellow CDC feather tips
Tail: Cream hackle fibers – split
Body: Creamy yellow
Hackle: Cream

Lawson's Spent Partridge Caddis

Hook: Dry fly #14-18
Thread: 6/0 Black
Body: Medium brown/olive or color to match natural
Under Wing: Clear Z-lon fibers
Wings: Tips of mottled partridge body feathers tied to curve out from the abdomen on each side
Thorax: Peacock herl
Hackle: Medium dun or to match natural

Tiny Blue Winged Olive

Hook: #20-24
Thread: Olive
Tail: Medium dun hackle fibers
Body: Dark brown olive
Wing: Short clump of snowshoe rabbit foot fibers

Trico – Spinner

Hook: #20-24
Thread: Black
Tail: Light dun microfibetts
Body: Male: gray black; Female: Pale gray-green abdomen and black thorax
Wing: Clear Z-lon fibers

Rusty Spinner

Hook: Dry fly #10-20
Thread: Brown
Tail: Dark dun Micro Fibetts
Body: Rusty brown
Wing: Light dun Z-lon or poly fibers

Sulphur Spinner

Hook: Dry fly #16-20
Thread: Yellow
Tail: Light dun Micro Fibetts
Body: Pale yellow or yellow and orange mixed
Wing: Light dun Z-lon or poly fibers

Olive Spinner

Hook: Dry fly #14-24
Thread: Olive
Tail: Dark dun Micro Fibetts
Body: Olive
Wing: Light dun Z-lon or poly fibers

Streamers

SLF Bugger

Hook: Streamer #4-12 mounted with gold bead
Thread: To match body
Tail: Marabou to match body
Body: Partridge SLF dubbing – place in loop and twist into chenille rope then wrap forward
Recommended colors: Black, brown, olive, blue and white.

Woolly Bugger

Hook: Streamer #4-12 mounted with gold bead
Thread: To match body
Tail: Marabou to match body
Body: Chenille
Hackle: Palmered from tail to head over body
Recommended colors: Black, brown, olive, blue and white.

Mickey Finn

Hook: Streamer #4-12
Thread: Black
Tail: None
Body: Flat silver tinsel or mylar
Rib: Oval gold
Wing: Yellow, red, yellow bucktail layered one on top of the other extending to the bend of the hook

Black Ghost

Hook: Streamer #4-12
Thread: Black
Tail: Yellow saddle hackle fibers
Body: Black floss
Rib: Flat silver tinsel
Hackle: Yellow
Wing: White saddle hackle
Eyes: Jungle cock (optional)

Muddler Minnow

Hook: Streamer #4-12
Thread: Black
Tail: Mottled turkey wing
Body: Oval or flat gold tinsel
Under Wing: Squirrel tail
Over Wing: Mottled turkey wing sections, matched
Head and Collar: Deer hair, spun and clipped

Toms River Bonefish Darter

Hook: Streamer #6-8
Thread: Tan
Eyes: Chrome bead chain
Body: None
Under Wing: Grizzly dyed tan or cree tied curving outward
Over Wing: Natural brown bucktail with three strands of pearlescent Krystal Flash on either side
Head: Medium root beer synthetic chenille

New Jersey Trout Stream Maps

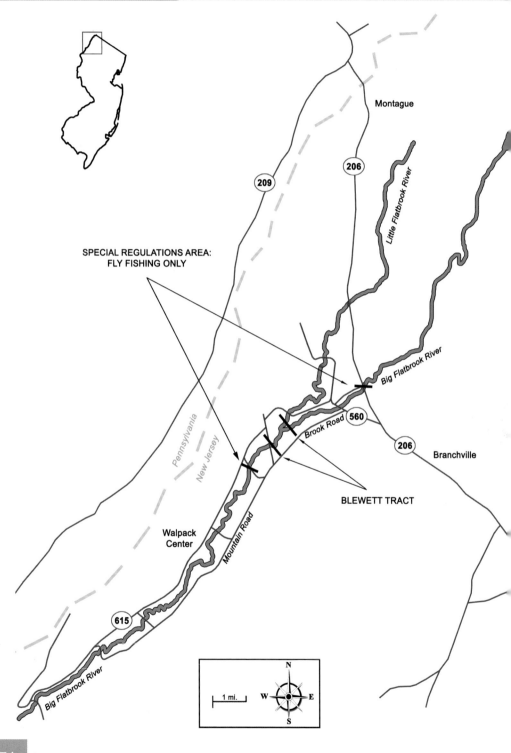

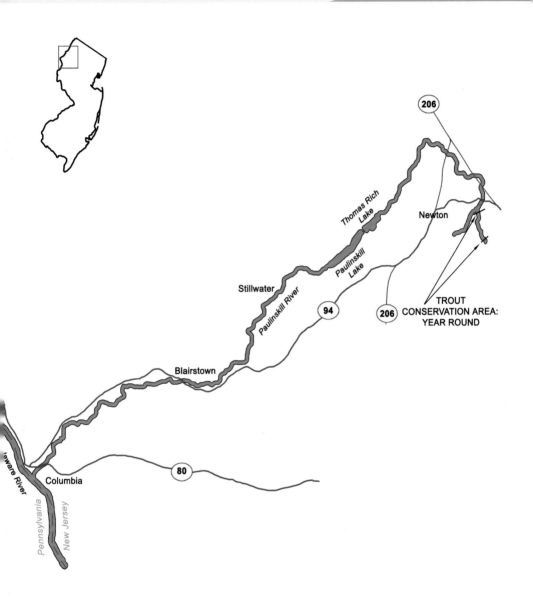

206

Thomas Rich Lake

Newton

Paulinskill Lake

Stillwater

Paulinskill River

94

206

TROUT
CONSERVATION AREA:
YEAR ROUND

Blairstown

80

Columbia

Delaware River

Pennsylvania

New Jersey

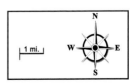

N
W ⊕ E
S
1 mi.

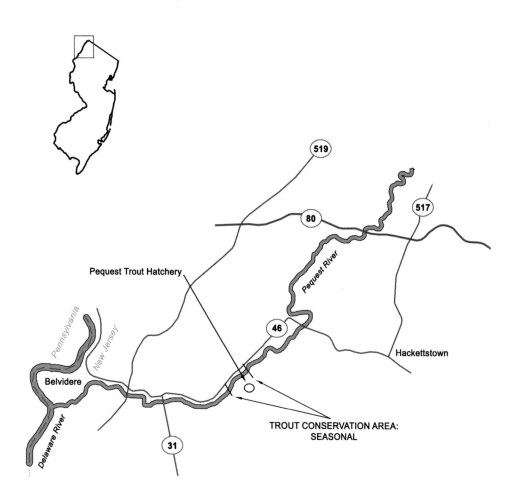

Pequest Trout Hatchery

519

80

517

Pequest River

Pennsylvania

New Jersey

46

Hackettstown

Belvidere

TROUT CONSERVATION AREA:
SEASONAL

Delaware River

31

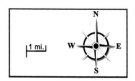

1 mi.

N
W E
S

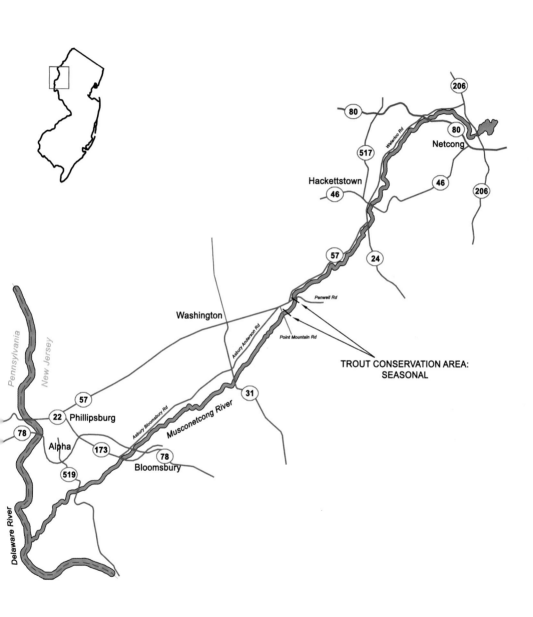

TROUT CONSERVATION AREA:
SEASONAL

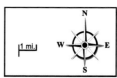

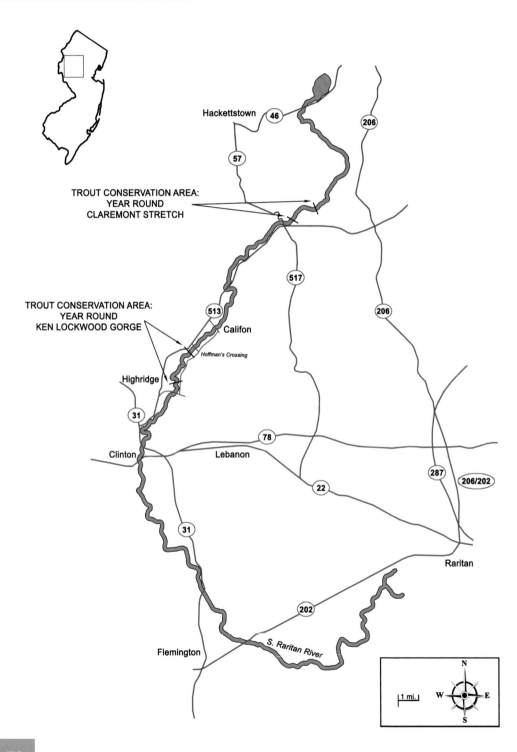

Hackettstown 46

206

57

TROUT CONSERVATION AREA:
YEAR ROUND
CLAREMONT STRETCH

517

TROUT CONSERVATION AREA:
YEAR ROUND
KEN LOCKWOOD GORGE

513

206

Califon

Hoffman's Crossing

Highridge

31

78

Clinton

Lebanon

22

287

206/202

31

Raritan

202

S. Raritan River

Flemington

N

1 mi.   W — E

S

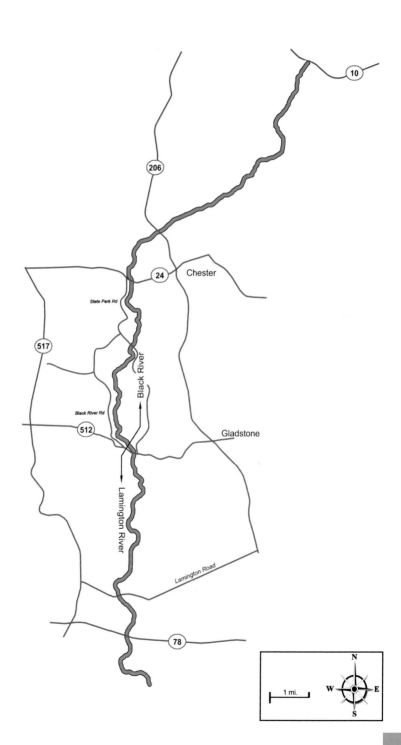

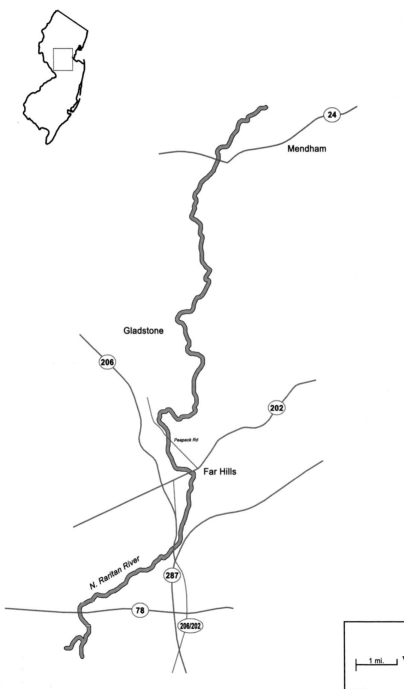

Mendham

Gladstone

206

202

Peapack Rd

Far Hills

N. Raritan River

287

78

206/202

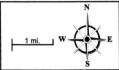

1 mi.

N
W E
S

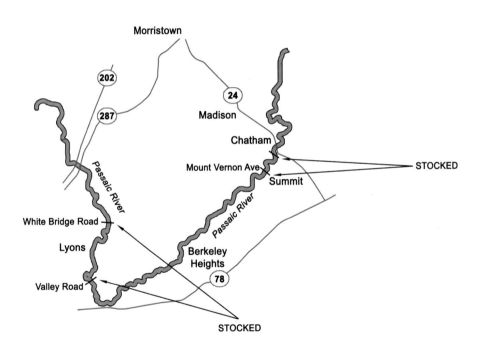

Morristown

202

287

24

Madison

Chatham

Mount Vernon Ave

Summit

STOCKED

Passaic River

White Bridge Road

Passaic River

Lyons

Berkeley
Heights

78

Valley Road

STOCKED

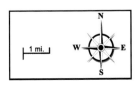

1 mi.

N

W — E

S

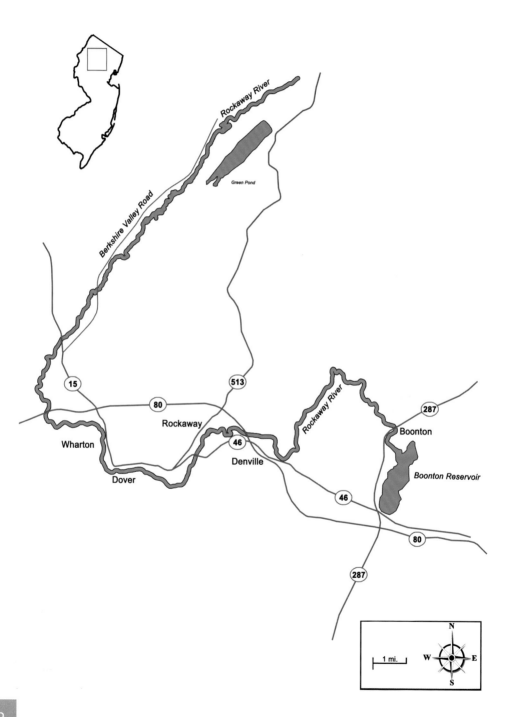

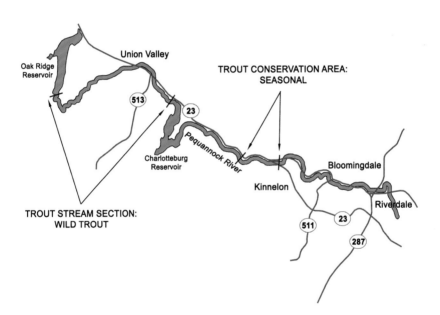

Oak Ridge Reservoir

Union Valley

TROUT CONSERVATION AREA:
SEASONAL

513

23

Charlotteburg Reservoir

Pequannock River

Bloomingdale

Kinnelon

Riverdale

TROUT STREAM SECTION:
WILD TROUT

511

23

287

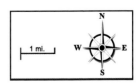

1 mi.

N
W E
S

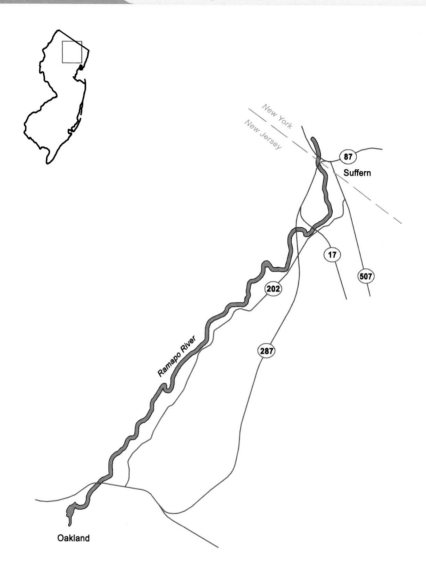

New York

New Jersey

87

Suffern

17

507

202

287

Ramapo River

Oakland

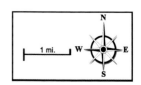

1 mi.

N
W — E
S

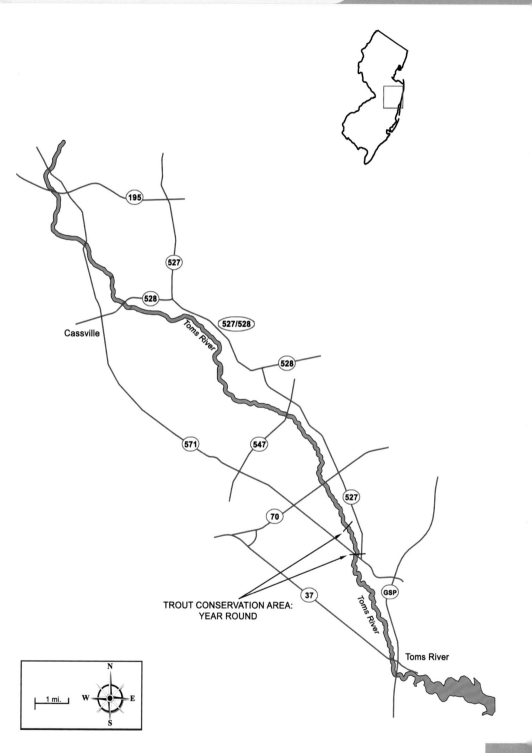

195

527

528

527/528

Cassville

Toms River

528

571

547

527

70

TROUT CONSERVATION AREA:
YEAR ROUND

37

GSP

Toms River

Toms River

N
W E
S

1 mi.

Resources

Internet Forums

NJ Trout
www.NJTrout.com
Site owner/administrator: Denis Ferfecki

North Eastern Fly Fishing
www.njflyfishing.com
Site owner/administrator: Dennis Cabarle

New Jersey State Agencies

NJ Department of Fish and Wildlife
www.state.nj.us/dep/fgw/index.htm
or www.njfishandwildlife.com

**NJ Department of Fish and Wildlife
– Places to Fish – Rivers and Streams**
www.nj.gov/dep/fgw/fishstrm.htm

NJ Department of Environmental Protection
http://www.state.nj.us/dep/

Other Useful Internet Sites

Wild Trout Streams of the Northeast
www.wildtroutstreams.com

Google Earth ™
Use it often to find new spots and find
that one place you can call your own.

Bibliography

These books have served as my constant references over the years and are well worn. I would be casting a short line though if I said they are the only sources of the fly-fishing data I have crammed in my head the last 35 years. So I want to give a blanket hatch of thanks and credit to the dozens of fly-fishing book writers that have come before me to fuel my passion for the sport. And that's my last piece of advice for every fly-fisher reading this—read, read, and read many more books on fly fishing and all that it encompasses. You never know when you will be on stream and a situation will arise that awakens something in your mind you read about that will suddenly make sense and lead to a successful outing.

ARBONA, FRED L., JR.
Mayflies, the Angler and the Trout
New York, New York: Lyons and Burford, 1989

CAUCCI, AL, AND BOB NASTASI
Hatches II.
New York, New York: Lyons and Burford, 1986

KNOPP, MALCOLM, AND ROBERT CORIMIER
Mayflies
Helena, Montana: Greycliff, 1997

LaFONTAINE, GARY
Caddisflies
New York, New York: Lyons and Burford, 1981

SCHWIEBERT, ERNEST G., JR.
Nymphs
New York, New York: Winchester Press, 1973

SCHWIEBERT, ERNEST G., JR.,
Matching the Hatch
Toronto: Macmillan, 1955

SCHWIEBERT, ERNEST G., JR.,
Trout.
New York, New York: E.P. Dutton, 1978

M atthew Grobert is a life-long resident of New Jersey. He has traveled the country extensively in search of trout and a better understanding of the rivers and their insects. He previously wrote the weekly "New Jersey Fly Fishing" column for *The Star Ledger*, "Beginners Corner" for the *Northeastern Fly Fishing Guide*, and has appeared in *Fly Fisherman* Magazine. He is an expert fly tier and has been teaching all disciplines of fly-fishing for 25 years. He lives in Summit, New Jersey.

Photo credits
From top to bottom:
Mark Sagan
Derek Martin
Matthew Grobert
Mark Sagan

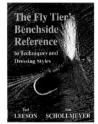

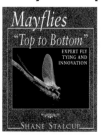